CH.A.D.D.

Educators
MANUAL

An In-Depth Look at
Attention Deficit Disorders
from an
Educational Perspective

A Project of the CH.A.D.D. National Education Committee

Written By
Mary Fowler

In Collaboration With
Russell Barkley, Ph.D.
Ron Reeve, Ph.D.
Sydney Zentall, Ph.D.

Published by CH.A.D.D.

Cover Design by: Sandra Redemske
Book Design by: Art Works

To
Sandra Freed Thomas
National President 1989-1992

YOUR VISION
AND TIRELESS EFFORT
WERE THE WIND
BENEATH OUR WINGS

---

and
for the children

Acknowledgements

The time, energy, effort and expertise of the following people made this manual possible. On behalf of the CH.A.D.D. National Board of Directors, we offer a debt of gratitude to one and all.

Author: Mary Fowler

Collaborators: Russell Barkley, Ph.D.
Ron Reeve, Ph.D.
Sydney Zentall, Ph.D.

Ms. Fowler is one of the country's leading education advocates for children with Attention Deficit Disorders, and the author of *Maybe You Know My Kid: A Parent's Guide to Identifying, Understanding and Helping Your Child with ADHD, 1990,* Birch Lane Press: New York. As National Vice-President of Federal Affairs for CH.A.D.D., Ms. Fowler is involved with legislative and policy issues concerning children with ADD. On behalf of CH.A.D.D., she works with the U.S. Department of Education, members of Congress, and representatives of other special interest organizations to ensure appropriate education opportunities for children with ADD. Ms. Fowler is the parent of a child with ADD and a former teacher.

Dr. Barkley, a clinical practitioner, scientist, and educator, is Director of Psychology and Professor of Psychiatry and Neurology at the University of Massachusetts Medical Center where he established the Center for Attention Deficit Hyperactivity Disorder. One of the country's leading ADHD researchers, Dr. Barkley supervises numerous ongoing studies on the disorder. He has published extensively, and is author of *Attention Deficit Hyperactivity Disorder: A Guide for Practitioners, 1990,* Guilford Press: New York. Dr. Barkley has produced two video cassettes for parents, professionals, and educators entitled ADHD: *What Do We Know?* and ADHD: *What Can We Do?*

Dr. Reeve is a psychologist and Associate Professor of Education at the University of Virginia where he has been on the faculty for the past 17 years. Dr. Reeve currently coordinates the School Psychology Program within the Clinical and School Psychology programs of the Curry School of Education. Dr. Reeve has a long history of involvement with children with ADD. For seven years he was part of the core faculty in the University of Virginia's Learning Disabilities Research Institute. He authored the influential Virginia Department of Education Task Force Report, *Attention Deficit Hyperactivity Disorder and the Schools,* which is frequently used for guidance by Departments of Education in other states.

Dr. Zentall is Chair of Special Education and Professor of Special Education and Psychological Sciences at Purdue University, Indiana. Her experience in the field includes teaching severely learning and behaviorally disabled children as well as teaching regular education classes. For the past 18 years, Dr. Zentall has been studying and publishing in the area of Attention Deficit Hyperactivity Disorders. Dr. Zentall is Immediate Past-President of the Division for Research at the Council of Exceptional Children.

Contributors:

Lauren Braswell, Ph.D., Clinical Assistant Professor, Department of Psychology, University of Minnesota, and Co-Investigator with the Minnesota Competence Enhancement Project funded by the National Institute of Mental Health.

Ross Greene, Ph.D., Assistant Professor of Psychiatry and Pediatrics, University of Massachusetts Medical Center.

Ron Kotkin, Ph.D., Program Director of the School-based Intervention Program for the Child Development Center at the University of California, Irvine.

Harvey C. Parker, Ph.D., Co-Founder of CH.A.D.D., Clinical Psychologist, and author of the *ADD Hyperactivity Handbook for Schools.*

Karen Rooney, Ph.D., Director of ADD Clinic, Learning Resource Center, Richmond, Virginia, and Adjunct Faculty, Department of Special Education, University of Virginia.

Terri Shelton, Ph.D., Co-Investigator of Prevention/Treatment Kindergarten Program and Assistant Professor of Psychiatry and Pediatrics, University of Massachusetts Medical Center.

James Swanson, Ph.D., Director of the Child Development Center, Professor of Pediatrics, Psychiatry, and Special Sciences, University of California, Irvine, and Director of one of the U.S. Department of Education ADD Centers. Dr. Swanson is President of the Professional Group for Attention and Related Disorders (PGARD).

A special note of thanks to JoAnne Evans, Chairperson of the CH.A.D.D. National Education Committee for encouraging this project and for her active involvement through all stages of the manual's preparation and publication.

Contents

Preface

Dear Reader,

CH.A.D.D. is a national non-profit organization comprised of parents, health care professionals, and educators. Our mission is to better the lives of individuals with Attention Deficit Disorders (ADD) and of those who care for them. Through family support and advocacy, public and professional education, and encouragement of scientific and educational research, CH.A.D.D. works to ensure that those with ADD reach their inherent potential. Since our formation in 1987, CH.A.D.D. has grown at a phenomenal rate. Today, we have over 350 chapters throughout the United States, with new chapters being formed daily. Efforts are currently underway to address the many requests CH.A.D.D. has received from other countries for affiliate status.

During the past three years, CH.A.D.D. has focused primarily on the task of improving the education of children with ADD. Our Washington, D.C. activities have resulted in a 1991 U.S. Department of Education policy affirming the obligation of state and local educational agencies to provide a free, appropriate public education to these children. Additionally, Congress has appropriated federal funds to improve the quality of in-service and pre-service educator training on ADD; and to finance several ADD centers to gather and disseminate information about this disability. Since the action taken by the Department and Congress, CH.A.D.D. has received numerous inquiries from the field about how to effectively educate children with ADD.

From CH.A.D.D.'s very beginning, educators have come to us looking for answers about what to do for the children suffering from this disability. Often, these teachers expressed the same frustration and sense of helplessness as we parents did. They saw children with potential not succeeding. They saw engaging children with lots of spirit gradually lose their spark, their eagerness, their self-esteem.

CH.A.D.D.'s National Education Committee undertook the project of producing the EDUCATORS MANUAL to provide the field with an in-depth look at ADD from an educational perspective. It examines *current* knowledge and information, as well as identification, assessment, and intervention practices in the educational environment. Yet, there remains much work to be done. We think the best practices are waiting to be developed by the professional educators. CH.A.D.D. hopes this manual will provide a good foundation and interim help for those trying to reach and teach our children with ADD. We look forward to its revision as the field experience unfolds.

This CH.A.D.D. EDUCATORS MANUAL has a point of view. Specifically, CH.A.D.D. considers parents, educators, and health care professionals as stakeholders with a vested interest in facilitating a positive outcome for children with Attention Deficit Disorders. Our empowerment comes from knowledge and understanding. Our solutions come from applying that knowledge and understanding in a problem-solving approach. As stakeholders, we must all see that these children do not remain disabled throughout their school years and inevitably into adulthood. Together we can and will build for these children a sense of competence and self-worth.

Mary Fowler
Author

Jeanne Evans
Chairperson
National Education Committee
October 1992

Section One

The Disability Named ADD

The Disability Named ADD

Attention Deficit Disorder is a hidden disability. No physical marker exists to identify its presence, yet ADD is not very hard to spot. Just look with your eyes and listen with your ears as you walk through the places where children are — particularly those places where children are expected to behave in a quiet, orderly, and productive fashion. In such places, children with ADD will identify themselves quite readily. They will be doing or not doing something which frequently results in their receiving a barrage of comments and criticisms such as, "Why don't you ever listen?" "Think before you act." "Pay attention."

We all know *who* these children are. It's just that we often don't know *why* these children are the way they are. And so we blame, punish, and ostracize them for "not getting with the program," when, in fact, these children are not programmed to get with the program. They are the children with Attention Deficit Disorders (ADD).

The term Attention Deficit Disorders encompasses two types of this disability: Attention-deficit Hyperactivity Disorder (ADHD) and Undifferentiated Attention Deficit Disorder (UADD). Children and adults with ADHD are hyperactive, impulsive, and have difficulty sustaining attention. Those with UADD have problems focusing attention, but although sometimes restless, this group does not exhibit the disinhibited/hyperactive behavior pattern characteristic of ADHD. Throughout this manual use of the terms Attention Deficit Disorders or ADD refers to both types unless otherwise specified. This disability is listed in DSM-III-R, the American Psychiatric Association's DIAGNOSTIC AND STATISTICAL MANUAL OF MENTAL DISORDERS, Third Edition, Revised, 1987. The DSM is a manual used by medical and mental health professionals to facilitate the

FACTS ABOUT ADD

Incidence

- affects an estimated 3%-5% of school age population
- present in females; prevalent in males by a three to one ratio
- continues to cause problems throughout adulthood in two-thirds of the cases
- is an equal opportunity disability which occurs across all socioeconomic, cultural, and racial backgrounds
- affects children and adults of all intelligence levels

Diagnosis

- based on symptoms observed in a variety of settings and documented by multiple sources
- medical procedures, such as blood and urine tests, EEGs, MRIs, and PET scans do not diagnose the disability
- requires differential diagnosis to rule in or out presence of other disorders based on evaluation
- often co-occurs with other disabilities, most commonly Oppositional Defiant Disorder (ODD), Conduct Disorder (CD), and Learning Disabilities (LD), but ADD *is not* the same as any of these disabilities

Treatment

- no known cure exists; problems arising from disability are treatable
- requires a multi-modal interdisciplinary treatment approach to assist child behaviorally, educationally, psychologically, and often but not always, pharmacologically
- students may require special education and related services designed to meet specific ADD needs which differ from needs caused by other disabilities

identification of adult and child psychiatric, learning and emotional disorders.

A Clinical Description of ADD

ADD is a neurobiological, developmental disability frequently characterized by developmentally inappropriate degrees of inattention, or overactivity, and impulsivity. These characteristics often arise in early childhood, are relatively chronic in nature, and are not readily accounted for on the basis of gross neurological, sensory, language, or motor impairment, mental retardation, or severe emotional disturbances. The defining features are typically associated with deficits in rule-governed behavior and in maintaining a consistent pattern of work performance over time.
(*Barkley, R.A. 1990. ATTENTION DEFICIT HYPERACTIVITY DISORDER:* A Handbook for Diagnosis and Treatment. New York: Guilford Press.)

To date, no one knows for certain what causes ADD. Evidence suggests, however, that a chemical imbalance or deficiency in certain neurotransmitters (chemicals affecting the efficiency with which the brain regulates behavior) may be at the root of the problem. Additionally, results from a 1990 landmark study conducted by Alan Zametkin, M.D., and his colleagues at the National Institute of Mental Health showed that the rate at which the brain uses glucose, its primary energy source, is lower in subjects with

---

FOR CONSIDERATION

Females with ADD tend to be less aggressive than males with ADD which may explain why fewer females are diagnosed. Given the absence of aggression, females and males have similar manifestations.

ADD. Evidence also suggests that ADD frequently results from a hereditary predispositon, and less frequently, from pregnancy and birth complications, acquired brain damage, toxins, and infections. Little or no valid support exists for the notions that ADD can result from

Diagnostic Criteria For 314.01 Attention-Deficit Hyperactivity Disorder

NOTE: *Consider a criterion met only if the behavior is considerably more frequent than that of most people of the same mental age.*

A. A disturbance of at least six months during which at least eight of the following are present:

(1) often en fidgets with hands or feet or squirms in seat (in adolescents may be limited to subjective feelings of restlessness)

(2) has difficulty remaining seated when required to do so

(3) is easily distracted by extraneous stimuli

(4) has difficulty awaiting turn in games or group situations

(5) often blurts out answers to questions before they have been completed

(6) has difficulty following through on instructions from others (not due to oppositional behavior or failure of comprehension), e.g., fails to complete chores

(7) has difficulty sustaining attention in tasks or play activities

(8) often shifts from one uncompleted activity to another

(9) has difficulty playing quietly

(10) often talks excessively

(11) often interrupts or intrudes on others, e.g., butts into other children's games

(12) often does not seem to listen to what is being said to him or her

(13) often loses things necessary for tasks or activities at school or at home (e.g., toys, pencils, books assignments)

(14) often engages in physically dangerous activities without considering possible consequences (not for the purpose of thrill-seeking), e.g., runs into street without looking

NOTE: *The items are listed in descending order of discriminating power based on data from a national field trial of the DSM-III-R criteria for Disruptive Behavior Disorders.*

B. Onset before the age of seven.

C. Does not meet the criteria for a Pervasive Developmental Disorder.

Criteria for severity of Attention-Deficit Hyperactivity Disorder:

MILD: Few, if any, symptoms in excess of those required to make the diagnosis and only minimal or no impairment in school and social functioning.

MODERATE: Symptoms of functional impairment intermediate between "mild" and "severe."

SEVERE: Many symptoms in excess of those required to make the diagnosis and significant and pervasive impairment in functioning at home and school and with peers.

Diagnostic Criteria 314.00 Undifferentiated Attention-Deficit Disorder

This is a residual category for disturbances in which the predominant feature is the persistence of developmentally inappropriate and marked inattention that is not symptom of another disorder, such as Mental Retardation or Attention-Deficit Hyperactivity Disorder, or of a disorganized and chaotic environment. Some of the disturbances that in DSM-III would have been categorized as Attention-Deficit Disorders without Hyperactivity would be included in this category. Research is necessary to determine if this is a valid diagnostic category and, if so, how it should be defined.

(Drawn from the American Psychiatric Association's DIAGNOSTIC AND STATISTICAL MANUAL OF MENTAL DISORDERS, 3rd edtion-revised, 1987.)

social or environmental factors, diet, or poor parental management. (Barkley, 1990)

Even though the exact cause of ADD has yet to be pinpointed, we clearly know that ADD is a neurologically-based problem. Children with the disability behave in a way that comes naturally to them. If these children are to be helped to minimize the effects of this disability, the adults in their lives must first accept that simple reality.

ADD Is Not A New Phenomenon

Despite the fact that ADD is one of the most common and widely researched of all childhood disabilities, there is much that scientists still do not know. Even so, public awareness lags far behind current research and clinical knowledge — perhaps with good reason. Over the course of the twentieth century, in attempting to understand and define the patterns of behavior frequently seen in children with ADD, researchers have renamed the disability to reflect theoretical advances and conceptualizations.

Children exhibiting characteristics of inattentiveness, impulsivity, and hyperactivity first received formal medical recognition in 1902 by British physician George Still. Dr. Still described these patients, who also had primary symptoms of aggression, disinihibition, and defiance, as suffering from a Defect in Moral Control. Although we now can find some humor in the profoundly Victorian nature of such a term, most parents and educators happily acknowledge its rather quick demise. Imagine how parents would react today at being told by a physician that their child is morally defective. In actuality, Still's use of the word "moral" referred to the ability to distinguish right from wrong and was not meant to imply a defect in one's character.

The MBD Era

The first half of the twentieth century witnessed the theory of brain damage, and later some type of central nervous system dysfunction as reasons why children exhibited characteristics of inattentiveness, impulsivity and excessive motor activity. Such children were said to have minimal brain dysfunction, MBD.

Eminent ADD researcher and author, Professor Russell Barkley at the University of Massachusetts Medical Center notes that the MBD term influenced the general acceptance of a neurological basis for the patterns of behavior frequently associated with ADD. The lack of defining characteristics, however, made MBD encompass too broad a spectrum of impairments to have much useful meaning for defining a given child's problems and developing an appropriate treatment plan.

As Time Marched On

By mid-century, hyperactivity came to be viewed as the primary problem of these children. This concept led scientific investigators to create a new diagnostic category, "The Hyperkinetic Reaction of Childhood" in the second edition of the Diagnostics and Statistical Manual of the American Psychiatric Association (DSM II). Since puberty often brought diminished hyperactivity levels, many people minimized the seriousness of the disability. It would go away, they thought, once puberty began. Though this view lasted less than a decade, the term "hyperactive" came into common usage and is often still used today.

Characteristics frequently associated with hyperactive children, such as impulsivity, short attention span, low frustration tolerance, and sometimes aggression, led the academic research community to conclude that problems with attention and impulsivity created the primary difficulties for these children. Hyperactivity gradually came to be seen as less central to the syndrome. The decade of the 70s thus paved the way for emergence of the term "Attention Deficit Disorder," first used in 1980 in DSM III. Since hyperactivity was not present in all children with attention difficulties, the diagnostic category contemplated both ADD with Hyperactivity and ADD without Hyperactivity.

During the late 1980s, the emergence of parent support groups concerned about ADD fostered public awareness of the disability. Then, just as the term "ADD" came to enjoy widespread use and public recognition, the disability again became redefined to reflect scientific advances. Researchers saw a vast distinction between children with hyper-

activity and those without this characteristic. ADD became Attention Deficit Hyperactivity Disorder (ADHD) in DSM-III-R. Attention problems without accompanying impulsivity and hyperactivity were categorized as Undifferentiated Attention Deficit Disorder (UADD). Pending further field investigation, scant information about UADD was provided in DSM-III-R.

Public Perception

The previously cited terminology changes were made to reflect increased scientific knowledge. Yet these name changes often frustrated lay persons trying to understand this intriguing, complex disability. A backlash of a sort ensued. Some people questioned whether ADD was a "legitimate" disability and raised the notion of intolerant parents and teachers labelling kids to make up for their own shortcomings. As evidence, items listed in the DSM were cited as behaviors all children exhibit from time to time. Those skeptical about ADD as a disability with potentially devasting effects failed to consider DSM-III-R key definitional criteria: the behavior (i) be developmentally inappropriate, (ii) occur prior to age 7, (iii) be prevalent for longer than six months, and (iv) not be attributable to childhood psychosis, autism or mental retardation.

The lay person needs to understand that ADD is a difficult diagnosis for clinicians to make. Later in this manual, identification and assessment protocols will be clearly defined, but for now it is sufficient to note that clinicians diagnosing ADD do not simply run down the DSM symptom list checking yes or no after items to determine whether a child has the disability. Instead, they use measurements with normative data, a careful developmental history, and observation in an attempt to define a general pattern of behavior indicative of the disability. Once that pattern is defined, they then rule out other possible causes for the behavioral patterns such as social and environmental stressors or pathologies.

Clearly, one might look only at DSM-III-R criteria list and find items that on occasion aptly describe many children's behavior, and perhaps the behavior of many adults as well.

ADD does not exist with the same intensity for all children diagnosed with the disability. Variations in degree of difficulty and level of severity are to be expected. Furthermore, since ADD has a neuro-biological basis and the human brain chemistry undergoes constant change, people with ADD will have variations in the degree of intensity of their symptomatology from day to day and even during the course of a given day.

FOR CONSIDERATION
From time to time all children will be inattentive, impulsive, and/or exhibit high energy levels. For children with ADD, however, this pattern of behavior is the rule, not the occasional exception.

Depending on the severity of the disability, children with ADD can be at significant risk for serious and long-term consequences resulting from their ADD characteristics.

The Shape of ADD To Come...

The fourth edition of the DSM is currently being written and due for publication in 1993. Once again we can expect changes. After collecting data and conducting field trials, the DSM IV Committee expects to continue usage of the term ADHD to describe children with problems with sustained attention, impulsivity, and hyperactivity. The term Undifferentiated Attention-Deficit Disorder will most likely be replaced by Attention Deficit Disorder. ADD will describe children with primary difficulties in selective and focused attention, but who are not hyperactive and impulsive. "We are certainly not changing the nature of the disorder or making substantial changes in the way it is described in the text," comments Dr. Barkley, a committee member.

As of this writing, the DSM IV committee expects to publish a two-dimension list of items for ADHD and a separate one-dimension list for ADD. Although the items probably will not be worded exactly as illustrated, the illustration below provides an idea of the nature of the behavioral manifestations likely to be included for diagnostic purposes. The number of items included is also subject to final committee approval.

ADHD
Two Dimensions
inattention
distractibility
disorganization
needing lots of supervision
not listening

impulsivity
fidgeting and squirming
difficulty remaining seated
running and jumping

•

ADD
One Dimension
inattention
distractibility
disorganization
needing lots of supervision
not listening
stares
daydreams
easily confused
lethargic
restless

In analyzing the types of items that will probably be included, you notice the two-dimension list indicative of an ADHD problem clearly illustrates two predominant patterns of behavior: difficulty with attention and difficulty with inhibiting behavior. "It is the difficulty with inhibiting behavior that really defines the ADHD group," Dr. Barkley explains. In the ADD group, however, attention and concentration difficulties without disinhibition are the defining features. Also, in the ADD group you see the general pattern of "spaciness." Note the inclusion of "restless" within ADD. Dr. Barkley further clarifies, "A little squirmy, restlessness is characteristic of ADHD *and* ADD, but we do not view that as hyperactive — as if driven by a motor."

Rationale For The Changes

The past ten years have witnessed a great expansion of knowledge in both the conceptualization and understanding of the population of children who were ADD with Hyperactivity and those who were ADD without Hyperactivity. Dr. Barkley explains: "The biggest difference in terms of the nature of ADHD versus ADD is impulsivity. For the ADHD group, the hallmark of the disability is this pattern of uninhibited/hyperactive behavior. The DSM IV Committee views ADHD as a disorder of disinhibition. Inattention exists, but primarily as difficulty with the persistence of effort and the motivational aspects of attention. Whereas, the difficulty for children with ADD lies more in the realm of selective and focused attention."

Disinhibition within the ADHD group explains one of the more frustrating aspects of parenting or teaching children with ADHD. These children seem to understand the requirements of a given task or situation. For instance, they pay attention to the assignment at hand, but don't stick with it to completion. Or they understand the social rule of not interrupting, but continually do so anyway. Rather than doing what they know, they often appear to act out or to be contrary deliberately.

We adults often view the lack of inhibition and stick-to-it-ive-ness as a choice made by the child. After all, a child who knows the skill, or the requirements of a given situation, should be able to follow suit. Yet, we must understand that the primary problem of these children is not in knowing the skill, but rather *in the ability to control impulse and apply the skill.* They do not have the option of choice.

"ADHD children are managed by the moment."

As Dr. Barkley so aptly describes, *"ADHD children are managed by the moment."* These children simply have a hard time waiting and regulating their behavior to the demands of a situation, or if you will, "getting with the program."

Children with ADD without the disinhibited/hyperactive behavior pattern also have difficulty "getting with the program," but in a much different way. Unlike the behaviorally impulsive ADHD type, once children with ADD know the requirements or the rules, they tend to follow them. It is, first, knowing what to pay attention to and, second, not losing or drifting from the focus of their attention, which are especially difficult for these children.

• The Little Engine That Didn't •

The more blame s/he received, the more he failed. The more he failed, the less he tried. The less he tried, the more he failed, until one day he just stopped trying. Then everyone said, "I told you so. The kid is lazy. Well, what did you expect? Parents don't care enough. Teachers don't try hard enough! The child is willful, obstinate. He could do it if he wanted to. He just doesn't care." Oh well! What did you expect?

FOR CONSIDERATION
Children of either subtype share a common bond. They are at the mercy of their ADD characteristics which are anything but user friendly. Left unrecognized as disabled or left untreated, they generally experience devastating consequences.

We Can Make A Difference

Serious academic failure and the inability to conform to the demands of the environment produce a far more debilitating outcome for these children than what statistics show. Over time they lose any sense of competence. Ultimately, they lose their sense of self-worth. These outcome have a staggering social and economic impact.

If we, the parents and educators of such children are to have any effect at all in changing the negative outcomes that result from this disability, *we* have to take the first step. That step is CHANGE OUR BELIEF SYSTEM. We must ACCEPT that ADD is a disability, and that these children behave in a way that comes naturally to them.

Knowledge about the disability coupled with the ability to readily identify its manifestations in a given child help parents and educators see that the *the child is in trouble, not the cause of trouble.*

Understanding that the child is in trouble and not the cause of trouble produces a change of attitude which becomes the cornerstone for all our efforts. How do you design an optimal program for the child with ADD? Dr. Ross Greene, Assistant Professor of Psychiatry and Pediatrics at the University of Massachusetts Medical Center says, "First you have to establish the level of understanding and knowledge on the part of everybody concerned. To the extent that knowledge, attitudes, and beliefs guid a person's behavior, these factors may have considerable impact upon a teacher's interactions with the student with ADD." In applying

CONSIDER
These Sobering Statistics About EDUCATIONAL OUTCOMES
For children with ADD:

From a study by Barkley et al. (1990) which followed children with the disability for 8 years.

- 30% had been retained in a grade at least once, with many retained more than once.

- 46% had been suspended, often more than once.

- 11% had been expelled.

- 10% had dropped out of school.

From longer term follow-up studies of children with ADD into adulthood.

- Over 50% retained in a grade at least once.

- 35% never complete a high school education.

- Only 5% complete college.

Weiss and Hechtman (1986).

Follow-Up Studies

Follow-up studies of children with ADD, in a variety of geographical locations spanning the United States, present a picture of *serious academic failure* for these children.

(Professional Group for Attention and Related Disorders, 1991. PGARD is an organization consisting of psychologists, psychiatrists, pediatricians, neurologists, and educators who have made a career commitment to investigate ADD.)

principles from the literature on parenting and behavior management practices to teaching, Dr. Greene notes, "There are behavior management practices that can be very counterproductive and damaging. For example, some people tend to react to children who do not follow directions by interpreting this behavior as willful and intentional. Consequently, they respond in a very punitive, heavy-handed manner. Responding this way to the child with ADD is likely to produce a negative outcome rather than the intended positive result."

FOR CONSIDERATION
The ultimate goal of all interventions is to help the child be competent, to do well in life, and to feel a sense of "I can!"

Section Two

ADD Goes
To School

ADD Goes To School

Introduction

We know that ADD creates school-related difficulties. In fact, problems occuring at school generally prove to be the catalyst for diagnosis and treatment. Yet, despite the heavy toll ADD characteristics exact from the child's ability to succeed in school academically and socially, seldom have these characteristics been viewed from an educational perspective. Knowing that a child is inattentive, and/or impulsive and hyperactive provides little understanding about the functional difficulties s/he experiences in the school environment. Unlike the previous section which explains the clinical side of ADD, this section delves into the how and why behind the educational difficulties created by ADD characteristics, and types of approaches that might effectively address the resultant problems.

Developmental Disability

ADD is a developmental disability. The defining features of inattention, impulsivity, and hyperactivity are reflected in behaviors inappropriate for a given child's age. Parents and teachers generally describe children with ADD as

> "ADD is not just a disorder within the child. Its expression depends on the match between the child and the environment."

immature. Whether the child's overall behavior pattern proves problematic to either parents or teachers varies according to situational demands and the child's developmental stage. In fact, parents and teachers frequently disagree over the existence of problem behaviors. Such disagreements do not mean that one party is right and the other mistaken. Age-inappropriateness must be viewed within the context of the environment.

As Dr. Ron Reeve, Associate Professor of Education at the University of Virginia notes: "ADD is not just a disorder within the child. Its expression depends on the match between the child and the environment. Behavioral difficulties may show up in school where demands are made for persistent effort. At home, the behavior may not look deviant, because there may be fewer task demands." Even when both parents and teachers agree that difficulties exist, they generally describe different behaviors as "the problem." Often, these disparities result from differing expectations and understandings about what constitutes age-inappropriate behavior.

Dr. Sydney Zentall, Chair of Special Education, from Purdue University provided much of the following developmental perspective which places a strong emphasis on how the defining features of inattention, and/or impulsivity and hyperactivity manifest themselves during the various stages.

Preschool Age

As the infant with ADD passes through the toddler stage and evolves into a preschooler, parents and teachers begin to notice behaviors somewhat deviant from the norm. At this stage, parents often describe the child as "demanding." Due to the hyperactivity and impulsivity, this child's quest for independence becomes a major concern for parents. Such children are highly accident prone. Accidents and a resistance to the development of routines tend to be the primary problems. Since the preschool environment allows for movement, inattention is seen through excessive motor activity and noisiness and in an inability to stay with play activities for sustained periods.

At this preschool level, parents report difficulties with increased activity and talking. Such behaviors prove even more bothersome when they occur in social contexts, such as at church or the din-

---

PARENTS REPORT:

excessive busyness

accidents related to independence

resistance to routines, e.g., brushing teeth, getting dressed

shifts frequently across play activities

talks too much

easily upset or frustrated

disruptiveness

noncompliance

aggressive in play

TEACHERS REPORT

more activity

more talking

less time spent on any single activity

noncompliance

ner table. Preschool teachers also cite increased activity and talking as problematic because preschool *is* a social context wherein the teacher is attempting to maintain a continuity. When the child does not stay with an activity, the class flow is disrupted. Additionally, impulsivity is reflected through noncompliance with class rules or teacher directions that involve waiting, taking turns, or being quiet while others have their say. Since increased activity is more predominant at this stage, children with ADD who do not have the impulsive/hyperactive pattern will not readily call attention to themselves as being deviant. They will, nonetheless, often be quietly off-task.

Elementary School Age

As these children advance through the elementary school years, demands for attention increase at home as well as in school. At this stage, parents and teachers are likely to report similar difficulties. Additionally, visual off-task behaviors become apparent to teachers. In general, children with ADD appear to channel gross motor movement into seat restlessness or fidgeting and looking around as they attempt to conform to situational demands.

Adolescence

By middle school, most of these children-turned-adolescents seem to have learned to channel their gross motor activity into fidgety, restless, visual off-task, or vocalizing behaviors. Hyperactivity is observed less frequently. Now, issues over independence claim center stage. These children do not glide into

PARENTS REPORT:	TEACHERS REPORT:
fidgeting, talking especially during homework	fidgeting
greater dependency on adults	out of seat
noisiness	requiring more supervision
interrupting	more talking
bossiness	interrupting
less sharing, rough play	off-task, especially visual off-task (looks about)
poor peer relations	bossiness
immature social interactions; few friends	erratic productivity
self-centered	intrudes on others activities
easily bored	poor persistence of effort

major developmental stages as easily as other children. Instead, they tend to spit and sputter. Accidents with potentially serious consequences prove more common among these children, such as auto accidents.

Additionally, their "trial-and-error" learning style tends to produce many academic and social problems. Except for those students with ADD who have developed the secondary problem of conduct disorder, the drama of adolescence diminishes somewhat during senior high years. Nevertheless, most students with ADD will continue to have difficulty performing to expectation and ability. Parents sometimes notice anxiety and depression in their teen-agers, particularly when school failure occurs. Parental concerns over the adolescent's self-control and judgment when away from home are prominent.

Adulthood

Preschoolers with ADD differ in their activity compared to non-ADD peers. Elementary school children with this disability exhibit more difficulties with social and academic tasks which carry into adolescence and compound over issues of independence. Adults with ADD continue having difficulty with tasks, only the

nature of the tasks changes from academic and social to work and life tasks. Adults with ADD often report difficulty sustaining jobs, relationships, and even residences.

Adults experience ADD-related difficulties differently than children because they have some control and choice, particularly with regard to the types of employment they seek. Their ADD-related difficulties are generally compounded by a lack of awareness about the specific disability they suffer. These adults often place themselves in job situations which make the same types of demands for sustained attention and impulse control as schools.

FOR CONSIDERATION

Children with ADD do *need* to look around more. You cannot assume that the child who is looking around is not listening to what is relevant. Nor can you assume that the child who appears to be paying attention is listening. That determination is made by asking the child questions.

FOR CONSIDERATION

The job for children and adolescents is school. There they get little, if any, choice. In fact, the very structure of schools tends to demand excellence in precisely those areas where these children do poorly.
(Dr. Reeve, 1992)

Academic and Social Difficulties

In thinking about how ADD characteristics affect educational performance, bear in mind that these children will generally experience difficulty in one or more of these areas:

- starting tasks
- staying on task
- completing tasks
- making transitions
- interacting with others
- following through on directions
- producing work at consistently normal levels
- organizing multi-step tasks

The following discussion of ADD characteristics offers possible explanations as to why problems occur in these areas. Pinpointing where problems arise provides a functional approach for designing interventions, and guards against expending energy in areas which are not problematic for a particular student.

The Attentional Process

Teachers often ask students to *"Pay Attention."* But what is the teacher really asking the student to do? What does it mean to "pay attention?" If a student

"Noticing a problem with attention is not enough. You have to find out what is driving the problem."

is looking at his work, is he paying attention? Well, he could be, but perhaps to the wrong details. "Noticing a problem with attention is not enough. You have to find out what is driving the problem," advises Dr. Reeve. He explains that the attentional process is comprised of a subset of skills.

To "pay attention," a student must:

1. FOCUS — *come to attention on something.* Focusing attention is the ability to pick one thing, usually the important one, to pay attention to. The child who has difficulty starting and getting into a task might have difficulty with focused attention. Such children can often complete tasks once they come to focus, but may make frequent mistakes as they fail to select out important from unimportant details.

2. SELECT — *choose the correct stimuli to focus upon.* The child with ADD has difficulty determining what is relevant. Such children may be busily processing many bits of information, but may not be focused on the central elements. These children tend to learn a lot of material, only the material they learn is either the wrong material, or they can tell you the parts of what they have learned, but not how the material interrelates.

3. SUSTAIN — *persistence of effort.* Sustained attention is the same notion as attention span. How long can the child stay focused? Some children are able to start a task without difficulty, but then prove unable to sustain. Since the natural state of attention is to wander, considerable effort is required to continuously return to things if they are tedious.

4. RESIST DISTRACTIONS — *to not be influenced by internal or external stimuli.* Can the child say "not now" to internal and external stimuli? These children may be pulled by whatever thoughts cross their minds, or stimuli that enter their sensory pathways.

5. SHIFT — *the ability to move attention on to a subsequent activity as the context requires.* Does the child have trouble leaving one task to start a new one?

It is necessary to observe the child's performance during tasks to determine which components of the attentional process are compromised. Of course, children can have difficulty with one or more of the components, and these components are interrelated. Yet, generally

speaking, children with ADD who do not have the impulsive/hyperactive pattern tend to have more difficulty with focus and selective attention (paying full attention to the important features of a task). The impulsive/hyperactive group appear to be more compromised in sustained attention (staying on and finishing tasks). Both groups may have difficulty resisting distractors (staying on and finishing tasks), although distractors may be problematic for different reasons. For example, the child with the impulsive/hyperactive type of ADD who finds a task boring or repetitive is less able to sustain attention and thus more easily drawn to distractions.

Impulsivity

Impulsivity can be separated into two domains: cognitive and behavioral. In differentiating the domains, Dr. Barkley explains that cognitive impulsivity refers to difficulty in stopping, thinking, and reasoning through a situation. Behavioral impulsivity is apparent in the inability to inhibit behavior or delay making a response. When researchers talk about children with ADD being impulsive, they are usually referring to behavioral impulsivity as opposed to cognitive impulsivity. Children without the disinhibited/hyperactive type of ADD are neither cognitively nor behaviorally impulsive as a rule. In fact, they are often sluggish or lethargic.

Behavioral Impulsivity

Children who do not wait, and who have difficulty delaying a response, rarely plan a course of action. Since they do not apply strategies to their learning and task performance, they appear to be cognitively impulsive, and therefore, skill-deficient. Educators naturally incline toward teaching such children cognitive skills designed to improve the approach to task. These efforts often prove futile, however, because *ADD is a problem of performance and not a skill deficit.*

Therein lies the source of consternation for many parents and educators. After the skills are taught and learned, the children do not use them. In Dr. Barkley's words, *"ADD is not a problem of*

> ## "ADD is not a problem of knowing what to do. It's a problem of doing what you know."

of knowing what to do. It's a problem of doing what you know." We must understand that behavioral impulsivity is the force driving such children away from the use of cognitive skills. These children with the impulsive/hyperactive type of ADD know what to do. They simply have difficulty taking the time to wait or delaying a response to do what they know before they act. Planning does not occur before performance.

Current Theoretical Perspectives

Dr. Barkley says, "Knowing what to do is a strategy problem. Doing what you know is a motivational problem." We usually think of unmotivated children as being lazy. But, as Dr. Barkley further notes, there is a neurological basis for the motivational difficulties in children with ADD. The frontal-limbic system, particularly the striatum, is believed to regulate inhibition and motivation. Recent brain-based studies on people with ADD indicate impairment in these areas. (interview with Barkley, 1992)

In terms of motivation difficulties, the profile of the child without the impulsive/hyperactive type of ADD differs from the child with this pattern. They tend to be behaviorally sluggish and often appear "spacey" or "lethargic." Children with the impulsive/hyperactive pattern, on the other hand, have lots of energy but disinhibition leads them to be managed by the moment. They seem to need immediate reward and pleasure and often prove unable to delay gratification. In neither case do these children *choose* to be governed by disinhibition and/or lack of motivation. Those traits are products of their neurobiology.

The notion that ADD may be a "motivational problem" has major implications for the way these children are viewed and the interventions we create for them. When the child with ADD does not use the skills learned, the tendency is to

believe the child is *choosing* not to use these skills. "You could do it if you wanted to, or if you tried hard enough," is an admonishment these children frequently hear. Once this disability becomes understood as a neurobiologically-based problem in motivation, the tendency to become frustrated by poor performance lessens. Instead, we become more inclined to find ways to increase performance.

Providing a lot of encouragement, motivation, and incentive has proven effective to achieve this end.

Getting Motivated

Stimulation is necessary to become motivated. But how much stimulation is needed is hard to say, because we each have different biological needs for stimulation. Some of us need much more stimulation than others. According to Dr. Zentall, "People who need more stimulation, do more to create it."

Dr. Zentall is one of the premier researchers from the field of education to study ADD. Based on her research, she believes that the children with ADD are seekers of stimulation, biologically driven to look for the novel and interesting. Unfortunately, what catches the child's attention is generally not the relevant information. "The ultimate goal for teachers of students with ADD," Dr. Zentall says, "is to channel stimulation seeking into cognitive tasks. Making school tasks moderately difficult and more interesting will help."

The idea that children with ADD are drawn to the salient perhaps explains the seeming disparities in the manifestations of ADD. Commonly we hear it said that these children appear to have difficulty paying attention, or concentrating for long periods of time, or even sitting still. Then they find something they enjoy like playing Nintendo; or something very stimulating like using bright markers to circle all the capitals of all the countries in the world on a classroom wall atlas. Once properly interested or stimulated, these children usually have no problem with finding the important information and persisting in these tasks.

Conclusion: These children can perform. That is precisely the point of Dr.

Zentall's and Dr. Barkley's perspectives. To do so, they require more enriching activities, clear rules and structure, and lots of rewards. They need the planning done for them, or else plenty of motivation to encourage their own use of planning.

The following pages of this section present Dr. Zentall's theories and research findings. (interview with Zentall, 1992) Her work illustrates some possible reasons for the poor performance characteristic of children with ADD.

Attentional Bias

Because children with ADD are seekers of stimulation, they have an attentional bias toward what is novel in the environment and within tasks. These children know what is salient or attention grabbing. But, they do not always know what is relevant because what is important in a task may not necessarily be the most interesting information. The stimulation then competes with the relevant task information. For instance, the child with ADD reading Hansel and Gretel would probably find the gnarly-fingered, hook-nosed witch who likes to eat little children the most important aspect of the fairy tale. If asked to identify the main idea, in all likelihood, this child would not have gotten beyond the exciting action of the witch to draw a conclusion.

In looking for the novel, these children will often miss neutral information in a task or situation. Thus, they need more

---

FOR CONSIDERATION
More behavioral disruptions will occur the longer a child is exposed to any particular setting or task. This happens because the child is basically satiated to that set of stimuli within the task or setting and, in an attempt to generate novel stimulation, inadvertently becomes behaviorally disruptive.

structure and routine. Transitions, which generally are not well-structured, prove especially difficult. Transition problems usually occur after the child has been sustaining attention for a period of time and ready for something more novel.

Attraction To Novelty

In thinking about the overall theme to the academic problems of these child-children, Dr. Zentall quotes Nietzsche. "Habit is a great deadener," he said. "These children do not want to deaden down. They want to interest up," she explains. Most academic problems are produced from tasks that require repetition, practice, or memory since learning in these tasks requires rehearsal.

Similarly, tasks that vary little are basically detail tasks. Since such tasks do not change much and therefore do not have novelty, these children have difficulty sustaining attention. Studies show that difficulty sustaining attention results in more errors and messier work on later performance, and increased activity over time (from morning to afternoon, from the beginning of a task to the end). The incidence of behavioral problems increases during repetitive, non-stimulating activities.

POSITIVE ACTION: Add novelty to the end of tasks. Delete repetition within tasks. Add activity to tasks, e.g., moving flip cards, working with peers, talking. Make tasks shorter. Develop routines for work completion, e.g., where to put material.

Difficulty Waiting

Children with both types of ADD appear to have an attentional bias toward novelty. In addition to being seekers of stimulation, the impulsive/hyperactive group, unlike their ADD peers without these characteristic are managed by the moment. They have great difficulty delaying and waiting to make a response, be it verbal or motor. This impulsivity poses numerous academic performance (productivity plus accuracy) problems, particularly in the following areas all of which require the child to wait before responding: organization, following directions, and planning.

POSITIVE ACTION: Dr. Zentall suggests giving the child something motoric to do while waiting to make a response.

The Teacher's Challenge

Children with ADD are *Learn By Doing, Trial and Error Learners.* They will learn to work for the following:

1. to get something (stimulating, active, novel)

2. to get out of or away from something (repetitious, boring)

Teachers of children with ADD face the challenge of how to incorporate more activity and novelty into their methods and materials. The following principles for remediation, based on Dr. Zentall's work, are recommendations which she submitted to the Council for Exceptional Children Task Force on ADD. They appear to apply to children of all ages.

Principles of Remediation for Excessive Activity

- Do not attempt to reduce activity, but channel it into acceptable avenues.
  - ☐ Encourage directed movement in classrooms that is not disruptive.
  - ☐ Allow standing during seatwork, especially during end of task.

- Use activity as a reward.
  - ☐ Give activity reward (errand, clean board, organize teacher's desk, arrange chairs) as individual reward for improvement.

- Use active responses in instruction.
  - ☐ Use teaching activities that encourage active responding (talking, moving, organizing, working at the board).
  - ☐ Encourage diary writing, painting, etc.
  - ☐ Teach child to ask questions that are on-topic.

Principles of Remediation for Inability to Wait (impulsivity)

- Give the child substitute verbal or motor responses to make while waiting and where possible do encourage day-dreaming or planning in the interim.
  - ☐ Instruct the child on how to continue on easier parts of tasks (or do a substitute task) while waiting for teacher's help.
  - ☐ Have the child underline or rewrite directions before beginning or give magic markers or colored pencils for child to underline directions or relevant information.
  - ☐ Encourage doodling or play with clay, paper-clips, pipe cleaners while waiting or listening to instructions.
  - ☐ Encourage note taking (even just cue words).

  Note: Dr. Barkley also suggests the teacher actively focus on and reward short intervals of waiting and gradually increase the length of the period.

- Where inability to wait becomes impatience and bossiness, encourage leadership but do not assume that impulsive statements or behavior are aggressive in intent.
  - ☐ Suggest/reinforce alternate ways (e.g. line reader, paper passer).
  - ☐ For children who interrupt, teach them to recognize pauses in conversations and how to hang onto ideas.
  - ☐ Cue child about upcoming difficult times or tasks where extra control will be needed.
  - ☐ Instruct and reinforce social routines (hellos, goodbyes, please, thank-you).

Principles of Remediation for Failure to Sustain Attention to Routine Tasks and Activities

- Decrease the length of the task.
  - ☐ Break one task into smaller parts to be completed at different times.
  - ☐ Give two tasks with a preferred task to be completed after the less preferred task.
  - ☐ Give fewer spelling words, math problems.
  - ☐ Use fewer words in explaining tasks (concise and global verbal directions).
  - ☐ Use distributed practice for rote tasks, rather than mass practice.

- Make tasks interesting.
  - ☐ Allow work with partners, in small groups, in centers.
  - ☐ Alternate high and low interest tasks.
  - ☐ Use overhead projector when lecturing.
  - ☐ Allow child to sit closer to the teacher.
- Increase novelty especially into later time periods of longer tasks.
  - ☐ Make a game out of checking work.
  - ☐ Use games to over-learn rote material.
- Do not teach or reinforce "dead-man's behavior"—that is, do not assume the child is not paying attention just because s/he looks out the window or at another child. Do not make on-task behavior a goal, without changing the nature of the task or learning environment.

Principles of Remediation for Noncompliance and Failure to Complete Tasks.

- Generally increase the choice and specific interest of tasks for the child.
  - ☐ Allow a limited choice of tasks, topics, activities.
  - ☐ Determine child's preferred activities and use as incentives.
  - ☐ Bring child's interests into assignments.
- Make sure tasks fit within child's learning abilities and preferred response style.
  - ☐ Allow alternate response modes (typewriter, computer, taped assignments).
  - ☐ Alter assignment difficulty level (give advanced level assignments or lower the level of difficulty).
  - ☐ Make sure disorganization is not reason for failure to complete tasks.

Principles of Remediation for Difficulty at the Beginning of Tasks.

- Generally increase the structure and salience of the relevant parts of tasks and social settings.
  - ☐ Prompt child for verbal directions (i.e., use written directions in addition to verbal ones; encourage note taking).

- ☐ Structure written assignments and tests (i.e., use graph paper for math; state standards of acceptable work being as specific as possible).
- ☐ Point out overall structure of tasks (topic sentences, headings, tables of content).
- ☐ Allow work with partners or in small groups with quiet talking.
- ☐ Color, circle, underline, or rewrite: directions, difficult letters in spelling, math process signs.

Principles of Remediation for Completing Assignments on Time

- Increase the use of lists and assignment organizers (notebooks, folders).
  - ☐ Write assignments for child in a pocket notebook.
  - ☐ Write assignments on the board. Make sure the child has copied them.
- Establish object-placement routines to retrieve routinely used objects such as books, assignments, and clothes.
  - ☐ Encourage routines of pocket folders with new work on one side and completed graded work and class notes organized chronologically on the other.
  - ☐ Encourage parents to establish places for certain things at home (books, homework).
  - ☐ Organize desk or locker with labels and places for certain items.
- Use color and physical/spatial organizers.
  - ☐ Before leaving one place for another (walking out of a door) teach routine of child self-questioning — "Do I have everything I need?"
  - ☐ Tape prompt cards in desks, on books, or on assignment folders.

Increasing Planning and Sequential Organization of Thought

- Practice planning.
  - ☐ Practice planning different activities (what is needed, how to break tasks into parts).
  - ☐ Practice estimating time needed for activities.
  - ☐ Teach outlining skills.

- Practice sorting, ordering, and re-ordering.
  - ☐ Teach the use of a word processor to reorder ideas.
  - ☐ Teach the child to take notes on lectures or on written materials in three columns (main points, supporting points, questions).

Principles of Remediation for Poor Handwriting.

- Reduce need for handwriting.
  - ☐ Do not have child recopy material. It will get progressively worse instead of better.
  - ☐ Allow student to copy a peer's notes or the teacher's notes.
  - ☐ Accept typed or taped assignments.
- Reduce standards on some assignments and make relevant standards clearer on important assignments.
  - ☐ Color, circle or underline parts of letters that children typically fail to close in cursive writing.
  - ☐ Allow reduced standards for acceptable handwriting.
  - ☐ Display particularly good samples of the child's work.

Principles of Remediation for Low Self-Esteem

- Generally recognize child's strengths and efforts.
  - ☐ Call attention to areas of child's strengths by allowing for a consistent time each day or week during which child can display his/her talents.
  - ☐ Recognize that excessive activity can also mean increased energy and productivity.
  - ☐ Recognize that bossiness can also be leadership potential.
  - ☐ Recognize that attraction to novel stimulation can also lead to creativity.
- Increase child's feelings of success by increasing child's skills.
  - ☐ Recognize these children's playfulness and use it to develop skills.
  - ☐ Mark student's correct performance, not the mistakes.

Section Three

Factors That Compromise Learning

Factors That Compromise Learning

Environmental Barriers

When thinking about how ADD affects the child's educational performance, environmental barriers must be considered. ADD is not just a problem within the child. The demands and expectations of parents, teachers, and situations often interplay discordantly with the child's ADD-related characterstics resulting in a lack of harmony. Given the innate difficulty these children have in meeting such myriad demands and expectations, educators face the crucial task of removing the environmental barriers. Otherwise, the behavioral problems of children with ADD become exacerbated.

Under certain environmental conditions, ADD-related difficulties tend to be less problematic. For instance, researchers note that, when observing children in a playground setting, hyperactive children will not readily distinguish themselves as more active than typical children.

Researchers also find that many of these children tend to be less behaviorally compromised when certain environmental characteristics are present in the classroom.

Some of those characteristics are:
- predictability
- structure
- shorter work periods
- small teacher to pupil ratio
- more individualized instruction
- motivating and interesting curricula
- use of positive reinforcers

Think about the typical behavioral demands made by many classroom teachers:
- Pay attention!
- Think before acting!
- Sit still!
- Finish work!
- Be quiet!
- Remain calm!
- Face forward!

These behavioral expectations do not allow for the special difficulties experienced by these children as a result of their ADD disability. Thus, many will fall short of performance standards.

Behavioral difficulties will also occur under these conditions:
1. when the task is difficult,
2. when work is required for an extended period of time, and
3. when there is little direct supervision.

Typical academic performance expectations also create barriers to success for these children. In U.S. public schools, generally all students are expected to do the same task in the same amount of time. As the years progress, students move from one teacher and shorter work periods to multiple teachers and longer work periods. During middle and senior high school, independence is expected. Students are changing classes. The curriculum becomes more information oriented and more often is delivered through lecture. The students are expected to find the relevant information *and* how it interrelates. Writing tasks increase considerably. Assignments are larger with longer time lines, and they require much more organization. Children with ADD tend to have serious difficulty in adjusting to this type of public school dynamic absent appropriate intervention.

Nor are environmental structure, demands and expectations the only factors interfering with educational performance.

FOR CONSIDERATION

As noted by Larry Silver, M.D., children with ADD are not unable to learn, but their difficulties with inattention and impulsivity often make them *unavailable* for learning.

Dr. Reeve explains that children with ADD do not process information reliably and efficiently. They rarely utilize learning strategies. Consequently, educational performance is impaired. To understand how the learning process is compromised, we need to delve into learning theory.

How Children Learn:

The Information Processing Model
(interview with Reeve, 1992)

Efficient information processing results in learning. In the information processing model, three basic processes are involved: input, short-term memory, and long-term memory. When information gets to long-term memory, it is learned. Once learned, the information is always there. A fourth process, output, is the expression of what is learned.

When thinking about learners with ADD, a key point to remember is that attention operates throughout the entire process, i.e., in the input, short-term memory, long-term memory, and retrieval-output phases. Thus, it is easy to understand that these children will have difficulty with one or more parts of the information processing system.

Following is a very rudimentary explanation of the operation of this very complicated process.

Input

We are constantly exposed to a vast array of environmental stimuli bombarding our senses. Each stimulus has a set of properties, e.g., color, intensity, uniqueness, and/or familiarity. We choose either consciously or unconsciously to pay attention to one thing out of this vast array and then select the most important features of the information. We must then sustain attention to that stimulus while inputting it using perceptual processes; visual, auditory, or tactile.

Children with ADD without the impulsive/hyperactive pattern will often not be aroused enough to focus (come to) attention. Thus, the input of stimulus will not occur.

Children with both types of ADD will have difficulty determining or sustaining attention to the relevant stimulus, i.e., what is important and what is not important. Consequently, even when attention is focused, often it is upon an irrelevant stimulus, i.e., not what the teacher is focusing on or the task at hand.

Short-Term Memory

Once a stimulus is inputted, we process the information in short-term memory, often viewed as the workbench of the mind. This part of the process is where attention problems really wreak havoc. Here, we must continue to pay attention to the information while working on it in preparation for long-term memory storage. Repetition and rehearsal are used to remember the information. For example, when we look up a phone number, dial, and get a busy signal, we generally rehearse the number, or write it down so it can be redialed without the need to look it up again. With more complex information, we must concentrate on the material long enough to figure out how to organize, categorize, or associate it with previously learned material. Children with ADD will have difficulty sustaining attention to the stimulus: in the non-impulsive group, possibly due to underarousal, while impulsivity probably interferes in the other group. Even those able to concentrate long enough can still have difficulty finding what's relevant and so they do not meaningfully organize, categorize, or associate information.

FOR CONSIDERATION

Children with ADD will be drawn away from the task to focus attention on a competing stimulus that is more interesting.

Long-Term Memory

Once material is rehearsed, organized, categorized, and associated, it is stored in long-term memory, the "file cabinet" or "computer memory" of the

mind. To retrieve information we must think about it. How efficiently the material was filed determines its accessibility and utility. When new information is introduced, we must recall previously learned material to short-term memory, associate the new material with the old, and then store this expanded file. Retrieval becomes easier as our associations increase. In order to remember information, we must make it meaningful. Meaningfulness is critical.

When presented with information, most learners use elementary techniques such as rehearsal or repetition for simple tasks like remembering a phone number. Making associations is another type of learning strategy. The student might ask themselves, "How does this material relate to previous information?" This strategy requires the learner to look at distinctive features of the information, and to try and figure out the inherent organization; for example, determining if a four-legged creature is an animal or a bird.

Output

In addition to processing information, many students with ADD will evidence difficulty with outputting information. Writing and spelling often prove to be their nemesis because of what these tasks involve. For most people, writing is a very natural process. When we listen to someone talk and take notes, the information flows through the listener/note taker to the paper. Children with ADD lose that flow of information. They do not move back and forth smoothly. They can either pay attention to what's being said, or pay attention to their writing. *Copying from the board is infinitely easier for them,* IF information is left there long enough.

Besides coordinating the flow of ideas with the flow of motor movements, writing requires remembering ideas, concepts, letter formation and spelling, while sequencing information, and following grammatical rules.

Some helpful hints include:
- teaching keyboarding skills and allowing computer usage,
- allowing extra time,
- making assignments shorter,
- teaching outlining skills,
- writing important notes to take on board.

Efficient information processing requires that the learner use learning strategies to make material meaningful. Research indicates that children with ADD do not employ learning strategies on their own. Rather than organize information, these children tend to scatter-shoot it. They do not automatically sift and sort information in logical ways. Because they bounce around attentionally between thoughts and ideas, they tend not to reflect on the structure inherent in the material. Ergo, these children characteristically can supply many details but may have difficulty explaining how details relate to one another.

Understanding that these children generally have great difficulty separating the forest from the trees is critical to improving their education. For the student with ADD, finding a main idea can be as futile and frustrating an experience as you or I might have in assembling a jigsaw puzzle without a box top picture. One suggested intervention principle is to first show the student with ADD the general information, or the whole picture, before working to the specific. For example, allow the student to read the Cliff notes on a lengthy novel prior to reading the book.

Certainly, impulsivity in ADD interferes with the child's use of learning strategies. Other, perhaps more interesting, stimuli intrude to pull the child off task. "I see the child with the impulsive/hyperactive form of ADD as having a lot of energy, but it's all over the place," notes Dr. Reeve. In contrast, he sees the other group as having difficulty with the intensity of arousal. "Even when they get aroused enough to energize the system, the arousal fades pretty quickly," he explains.

Inefficient information processing also leads to inconsistency of performance. Here, inconsistency is not to be confused with the difficulty of persistence of effort over time, which is characteristic of many of these children. Instead, inconsistency resulting from inefficient information processing is reflected in the child who may remember material one day and not be able to recall it the next. Often such children are accused of not trying hard enough or deliberately not paying attention. Because they process inefficiently, they generally do not have the slightest idea of why they cannot remember.

They may even have difficulty remembering material within a class period. The child with ADD might raise a hand for the entire class period, finally get called on, fail to remember why the hand was up, and then make funny noises instead. Such behavior is interpreted as willfully disruptive; the teacher admonishes the child; classmates snicker, and the teacher says, "Everybody settle down." Although perhaps feeling stupid and foolish, the child also reaps some reward by being a class clown. Nevertheless, the root of the child's difficulty goes unrecognized.

Implications For Educators

There are two circumstances under which children with ADD will be enabled to process information reliably and efficiently:

1. when relevant information is salient. This means that the critical information within lessons and tasks has to be highlighted in some fashion.

2. when techniques and strategies are incorporated to make information meaningful.

Regardless of whether the teacher is dealing with the ADD action-oriented

FOR CONSIDERATION
Although most learners can succeed without being taught strategies, most children with ADD cannot survive without them.

learner or the underaroused type learner, the remedy is much the same. "You want to be sure that the important stimuli look more intriguing," Dr. Reeve says. He recommends intensifying the stimulus by saying it louder or markedly softer, using color or size differences in print or with pictures, and providing more organization to help the student make the associations. To do so, the teacher will need to bring more energy to the task, and/or make the task more interesting. Making

Strategies for Efficient Information Processing
Memorization/Association

1. Have the students read the information to be memorized out loud into a tape recorder that can be used as an audio study tape while looking at the information.
2. Have students draw diagrams or pictorials for information to be memorized.
3. Teach mnemonic strategies, e.g., HOMES for the Great Lakes (Huron, Ontario, Michigan, Erie, Superior).
4. Have students describe the information to be memorized verbally to focus attention on important detail.
5. Have students make mental pictures to support memorization of information.
6. Have students put chunks or parts of the material to be learned (i.e., a poem) on separate cards so that a manipulative system for study results.

Organization of Instruction

1. Present the concept as well as the component parts but use a different color for the concept that is being identified so the concept will be highlighted.
2. Break work down into manageable units. For example, 40 math problems can be presented better by cutting the paper into four sections so the student only has to complete 10 at a time which increases their opportunities for task completion.
3. Emphasize critical pieces of instruction by highlighting their importance through the use of color, visual borders or highlighting.
4. Include attention or stretch breaks in the lesson plan.
5. Use pair instruction for classwork so partners can work together.
6. Underline key phrases and words in directions.
7. Have students repeat or rephrase directions.
8. Use modeling and demonstration rather than oral presentation.
9. Utilize computer-assisted programs when possible.
10. Use visual organizers to provide visual structure for oral presentations or assignments.
11. Make sure students have review systems or material at the conclusion of the instruction.
12. Get a sample of the student's understanding of the lesson that was presented.
13. Build the necessary vocabulary for comprehension in a content area rather than depend on prior knowledge.
14. Teach organization strategies to provide a model for how work can be completed or studied. Emphasize the process as well as the content.

Provided by:
Karen Rooney, Ph.D. and Director of the Learning Resource Center in Richmond, Virginia.

material more interesting and organized provides the motivational value for the impulsive/hyperactive learner with ADD and more clarity about what material is relevant for the underaroused other type of ADD learner.

It is important to note that teaching and modeling learning strategies will benefit all students and will make learning interactive.

Notes

Section Four

Identification
and
Assessment

Identification and Assessment

The School's Role

"In the majority of cases, concerns about a child's attention and activity levels will arise first in the context of school. This occurs because school places greater demands on the child than s/he previously experienced both for duration and intensity of attention. In other cases, parents will be the first to express concern, but they will indicate their concern to school personnel rather than proceeding directly to a physician. How should the situation be handled by school personnel?"
(Virginia Department of Education Task Force Report on ADD)

The U.S. Department of Education recently determined that ADD is a disability to be served under the federal category of "other health impaired" in U.S. Public Law 94-142 (Individuals with Disabilities Education Act), and under Section 504 of the Rehabilitation Act. This new Department ADD policy has generated the need for assessment protocols for school-based evaluation teams. This section includes recommendations made in the Virginia Department of Education Task Force Report on ADD, and also by PGARD, the Professional Group for Attention and Related Disorders whose members include the leading U.S. psychologists, psychiatrists, pediatricians, neurologists and educators professionally involved with ADD research. The combined Virginia/ PGARD assessment protocol put forth for ADD is based on sound clinical and educational practice.

The Purpose of Assessment

In keeping with evaluation requirements of Part B of IDEA, when a child is suspected of having or diagnosed with ADD, schools have an affirmative obligation to evaluate that child to determine or confirm the presence of the disability and the adverse affect it has on the child's educational performance.
(U.S. Department of Education Policy Clarification Memorandum on ADD, 9-16-91. See appendix).

Who Should Conduct The Assessment

Public Law 94-142 requires that the school-based multidisciplinary teams conduct the assessment of all children with disabilities including those with ADD, of all children suspected of having a disability including those suspected of having ADD, and to evaluate how a disability adversely affects the child's educational performance. A teacher's assessment, by itself, does not sufficiently comprise a thorough and proper evaluation. Assessing children with ADD requires input from psychoeducational personnel who have the following characteristics:

a. training in child psychopathology in order to make differential diagnoses among child psychopathological and psychoeducational disorders,

b. appropriate experience to evaluate how stressful family and life events may impact upon child adjustment,

c. demonstrated sensitivity about racial, ethnic, cultural, socioeconomic status, and linguistic factors which may bias assessments of minority children.

Such personnel are most likely to be school psychologists *with training in the assessment and management of ADD.* Other appropriate personnel include school social workers (or visiting teachers acting in that capacity), additional educational staff who routinely evaluate children with other IDEA Part B disabling conditions, and the child's teacher or teachers. Outside physicians or psychologists acting as consultants may also be needed to assure accurate assessment and evaluation.

TRAINING NEEDED

To conduct a proper assessment, educational personnel must have adequate training in the general psychoeducational assessment of children, in the specific psychological assessment of ADD, and in the use of non-standard procedures for assessing students who may be subject to bias due to racial, ethnic, cultural, or socioeconomic factors. When needed, such training can be provided through pre- and in-service training programs, or continuing education workshops.

Differential Diagnosis

Determining if a child has ADD is a multi-faceted process. Many neuropsychological or physical problems and psychosocial stressors can either directly or indirectly result in the behavioral symptoms of inattentiveness, impulsivity, excessive activity, or fidgeting. Thus, when a child is referred for behavioral difficulties which can be categorized under these broad constructs, the evaluator must proceed carefully. No definitive medical test exists to determine if a child does or does not have ADD. This diagnosis is made on the basis of information gathered about behavioral symptoms identified from a variety of sources/ evaluations.

The legal standard for determining whether a child has ADD is based upon whether the child's disability is diagnosed according to DSM-III-R. The challenge for evaluators is to rule in and rule out competing diagnoses. Dr. Ron Reeve, author of the Virginia D.O.E. Task Force Report on ADD, Coordinator of School Psychology at University of Virginia, and a PGARD member, explains: "If a child is demonstrating age-inappropriate levels of inattention, impulsivity or hyperactivity and has 8 to 10 of the 14 DSM-III-R criteria, you do not assume the child has ADD. Instead you assume the child *could* have ADD."

The presence of behaviors on the DSM-III-R list are necessary for the diagnosis of ADD, but not sufficient to make it. Evaluators must consider competing diagnoses which could share the same symptomatology. Dr. Reeve describes the following conditions with similar symptomatology with which ADD is commonly confused.

Central Auditory Processing Disorder

Central Auditory Processing Disorder (CAPD) is a disorder of perception, sound, and language. Children with CAPD are described as "poor listeners," have short auditory attention spans, appear unable to sustain attention to a task, and have trouble following directions, especially in noisy or acoustically poor settings. These children frequently have high levels of activity, although some are less active than normal to the point of lethargy. Some children with CAPD can't hear certain tones, but more typically, language processing is confused. Thus, words and phrases are misordered. Often the children will speak as they hear. They end up not paying attention when someone is talking to them, because they do not get the information needed auditorially and have learned to tune out. History of severe or recurrent otitis media may be an indicator. CAPD is readily diagnosed with specialized equipment used by specially trained audiologists. If suspected, observe the child to determine if s/he is paying attention when not relying on auditory processing. This would suggest CAPD rather than ADD.

Anxiety and Depressive Disorders

Although scientific evidence suggests a familial or genetic predisposition to axiety and depression, childhood anxiety and depression are commonly considered as the result of a stressful event the child has experienced. Such stressful events could be the death of a loved one, parental divorce, physical, sexual or emotional abuse, environmental disrup-

tion (change in residence or school), or natural or man-made disasters. Symptoms of inattention, impulsivity, and over-activity will arise suddenly. In such cases evalutors should look for a sudden change in behavior in response to an emotionally distressing event. Of course, children with ADD could also experience stressful life events that exacerbate the disorder. History typically will reveal evidence of cardinal features prior to such stressful life events for children with ADD.

Chaotic Home Environment

Children from disordered or chaotic home environments may have difficulty sustaining attention and behaving in a goal oriented fashion. This issue can be more problematic and more prominent for children upon first entering school. If they have not been exposed to structure, and have no models for it, they are likely to perform haphazardly. Certainly, effects of a disordered home environment might not be evident until the child reaches a point in school where organizing and planning skills are required to negotiate through the school day. If a disordered environment is determined, structure within the school should be provided to see if performance improves. Of course, children with ADD could have chaotic home environments as well, although this is usually found more in the cases of children with Oppositional Defiant Disorder.

Co-Morbidity

A companion notion to differential diagnosis is co-morbidity. It is quite possible that children with ADD will have more than one disability. This point is important for evaluators to consider since disabilities are not mutually exclusive. According to Dr. James Swanson, Director of the U.C. Irvine Child Development Center and President of PGARD, usually the most severely affected children with ADD will have coexisting disorders.

Estimates based on research studies suggest that approximately 25% of children with ADD have co-occuring learning disabilities. Oppositional Defiant Disorder (ODD) is apparent in 40–60% of elementary age children. Roughly 20–30% develop Conduct Disorder (CD). When severe or profound mental retardation (MR) is present, ADD is generally not considered as a co-occuring diagnosis.

When mild to moderate MR is present, however, ADD is considered, provided the child's inattention is significantly deviant when compared to others of the same mental age. (American Psychiatric Association, DSM-III-R, 1987; Barkley, 1990)

Because public school service delivery systems may all too often be tied to categorical labels, school-based assessment teams often look for disabilities on an either/or basis rather than determining co-morbidity. The two most common situations in which this issue arises involve specific learning disabilities (SLD) and serious emotional disturbance (SED). (The following information is paraphrased from the PGARD response to the U.S. Department of Education Notice of Inquiry mandated by the U.S. Congress, 1991.)

Why ADD Is Not SLD

ADD has long been confused as a subtype of learning disabilities. In distinguishing ADD from SLD, many studies show that children with ADD do not have deficits on tests of language function on which children with SLD demonstrate their greatest deficit, such as tests of word recognition, word attack skills, verbal memory, and verbal comprehension. (August & Garfinkel, 1990; Douglas, 1983; Douglas & Benezra, 1990; Douglas & Peters, 1978; Feiton et al., 1987; Pennington, 1990; McGee et al., 1989)

Furthermore, studies of the SLD discrepancy criterion in children with ADD have shown that in the vast majority, these children do not show a discrepancy between intelligence and academic

---

KEY POINTS

Distinguishing ADD from SLD

- Inattention and impulsivity associated with ADD are not the result of a language processing problem.

- Ability/achievement discrepancy formulas are not an accurate measure of the educational impairment of children with ADD.

- ADD adversely affects educational performance in terms of productivity and accuracy of work completed.

---

achievement in an area of basic academic skills such as reading, arithmetic, or spelling as measured by well-standardized achievement tests. (August & Garfinkel, 1990; Barklely, 1990; Lambert & Sandoval, 1980)

Instead, *children with ADD show a discrepancy between their intelligence and their academic productivity and work accomplishment.* Other studies have found that children with ADD are rated as considerably more deviant on behavior rating scales measuring inattentive, overactive, and impulsive behaviors by their teachers than are children with SLD. (Breen & Barkley, 1984)

These findings are consistent with numerous other studies concluding that ADD differs from SLD because of the former's significant inattention and impulsivity which are not essential characteristics of SLD, while the latter's language-based and/or perceptual deficits are not essential characterists of ADD.

Why ADD Is Not SED

Numerous studies document that children with ADD do not routinely manifest the characteristics of SED as part of their disorder. Further, children with ADD manifest a performance deficit instead of an "inability to learn," which is one of the IDEA criteria for SED. Because of inattention and impulsivity they engage in off-task activities in many situations when educational material is being presented to them or when school work is required of them. As a result, children with ADD may perform poorly in school but for very different reasons than children with SED.

In addition to an inability to learn, SED

KEY POINTS

Distinguishing ADD from SED:

- ADD is not characterized by a pervasive mood of unhappiness or depression; however low self-esteem often results due to academic and social failure.

- The capability and skills are present to initiate satisfactory interpersonal relationships with peers and teachers, and over half of the children with ADD can maintain friendships.

- Most of the children with ADD do not have coexistent psychiatric disorders associated with emotional distress (e.g., affective disorder, anxiety disorder) or qualitatively abnormal cognitive or social abilities (e.g., as in schizophrenia).

is manifested in the following ways: an inherent inability to build or maintain interpersonal relationships with peers or

PGARD Educational Description

NOTE: *Since the DSM-III-R criteria were developed for use in clinical practice and do not specifically emphasize the manner or degree to which ADD impacts educational performance, PGARD developed this educational description for guidance in educational assessment.*

The condition "attention deficit disorder" (ADD) refers to a developmental disorder involving one or more of the basic cognitive processes related to orienting, focusing, or maintaining attention, resulting in a marked degree[1] of inattention when engaged in academic tasks and social interactions. This disorder may also include verbal or motor impulsivity and excessive non-task related activity, such as fidgeting or restlessness. The inattentive behavior of ADD most commonly has onset in early childhood[2] remains inappropriate across age-related changes, and persists throughout development.

ADD adversely affects educational performance to the extent that a significant discrepancy exists between a child's intellectual ability and that child's productivity with respect to listening, following directions, planning, organizing, or completing academic assignments which require reading, writing, spelling, or mathematical calculations.

Inattentive behaviors, if caused by cultural or linguistic differences, socioeconomic disadvantages, or lack

teachers, or "inappropriate" types of behaviors or feelings under "normal" conditions or a generally pervasive mood of

of adequate exposure to educational instruction, are not evidence of ADD. Inattentive behaviors with acute onset are not evidence of ADD if they arise from (1) stressful events associated with family functioning (e.g., parental divorce, or the death of a family member or close friend) or environmental disruption (e.g., a change in residence or school); (2) posttraumatic stress reactions caused by abuse (e.g., physical, psychological, or sexual) or natural disasters; (3) non-compliance due solely to opposition or defiance; (4) frustration resulting from inappropriate tasks beyond intellectual ability or level of academic achievement; (5) emotional disorders (e.g., anxiety, depression, schizophrenia) or physical disorders (e.g., epilepsy, head injuries, sickle cell anemia, etc).

ADD can coexist with other disabling condition (i.e., specific learning disabilities, serious emotional disturbance, or mental retardation).

[1] "a marked degree" means, at a minimum, disproportionate for the child's age — as measured by well-standardized and unbiased rating scales or structured interviews — which results in functional impairment.

[2] "onset in early childhood" means that when a careful developmental history of the child is obtained, it confirms that parents, teachers, or other involved adults have observed the development of age-inappropriate inattentive behaviors before the age of 7 years. The onset of these persistent inattentive behaviors should not be confused with the educational manifestations of ADD, because onset of educational impairment may occur at any time in the child's life when school tasks tax the child's underlying attentional deficit.

This educational description is divided into three parts. The first paragraph defines ADD as primarily a disorder of inattention, and possibly verbal or motor impulsivity and excessive non-task related activity. The early onset and pervasiveness criteria are included to emphasize that sudden onset of inattention and other associated behaviors may indicate difficulties other than ADD. The second paragraph addresses the issue of how the disorder adversely affects educational performance by analyzing discrepancies between intellectual ability and productivity. The third paragraph describes sociocultural and socioeconomics factors, in addition to psychopathologies and psychostressors that might result in the child's displaying inattentive, impulsive, or excessively active behaviors. Such behaviors would not likely reflect ADD under the circumstances described here. Finally, the issue of co-morbidity is emphasized.

unhappiness or depression or a greater incidence of physical or emotional symptoms of anxiety disorders or childhood schizophrenia.

Many children with ADD may be more emotional than children without disabilities, but the emotional displays of children with this disability are clearly reactions to immediate environmental **events and closely tied to the reality of the moment. (Barkley, 1990; Carlson, 1990; Nieman & De Long, 1987). Studies that have followed children with ADD for 10 to 20 years have not found them to display significant degrees of depression relative to normal control groups. Many of these children with ADD do report feelings of low self-esteem resulting from their failure to achieve success academic and social environments, while in SED, a pervasive mood of unhappiness or depression is thought to be the cause of such failure. (PGARD, 1991)

FOR CONSIDERATION
Because of confusion about these categorical labels and their relationship to ADD, it is necessary to differentiate SLD and SED from ADD.

PGARD Recommended Assessment Protocol

In evaluating children suspected of or diagnosed as having ADD, PGARD proposed that school-based personnel follow a two-tiered approach. *Tier One* of the evaluation is to confirm that the child has ADD by determining the presence of the cardinal characteristics, early onset,

chronic duration, and exclusionary criteria. (A prior diagnosis by a competent physician or psychologist can be used in lieu of Tier One.)

Tier Two is used to determine adverse impact on educational performance. Information gathered during this stage would determine impairment of academic productivity (i.e., amount of work performed within a fixed time period and percentage of work completed correctly) and social interactions with school personnel and peers (i.e., percentage of time on playground spent in positive, negative, or no interactions) relative to other children of same ethnic and cultural background, and of the same chronological or mental age.

Using Multiple Sources of Information is the guiding principle underlying both tiers of assessment. Since no definitive medical test exists, the evaluation team must acquire much information to make an accurate determination.

FOR CONSIDERATION
- ADD is present in varying degrees of severity.
- These children are not equally disordered across all situations. (Problems are generally apparent when the information load is high, or when the child is required to work for extended periods of time without supervision.)
- There is no prototypic ADD child.

TIER ONE
Determining Presence of ADD Symptomatology

- Home, School and Community Information
- Rating Scales

TIER TWO
Determining Adverse Affect on Performance

- Classroom Observation
- Academic Productivity
- Psychoeducational Tests
- Measures of Attention

Key questions evaluators will want to answer include:

1. Does the child exhibit a significant number of behavioral symptoms of ADHD according to parent and teacher report?

2. Does the child exhibit ADHD symptoms at a frequency that is significantly greater than that demonstrated by children of the same gender and mental age?

3. At what age did the child begin demonstrating ADHD-related behaviors, and are these behaviors currently evident across many situations?

4. Is the child's functioning at school, at home, and with peers significantly impaired?

5. Are there other possible deficits or factors which could account for the display of ADHD symptoms?

(DuPaul, G. (1992). How to assess attention-deficit hyperactivity disorder within school settings. School Psychology Quarterly, Vol. 7, No. 1, 60-74.)

TIER ONE
Determining Presence of ADD Symptomatology

Home, School and Community Information

☐ _Comprehensive Interview with Parents or Guardians_
PURPOSE:
  a. determine if core features are present, age of onset, chronicity, pervasiveness, information about competing diagnoses, psychosocial stressors
  b. document relevant events from child's medical, developmental, social, and academic history
  c. denote particular details of child's ADD characteristics within home, especially the impact upon performance of school homework and academic study habits.

☐ _Comprehensive Interview with Instructional Personnel_
PURPOSE:
  a. determine existence of core features in current academic placement (emphasis placed on types of ADD-related characteristics manifested in academic work — amount produced and accuracy — and social interactions within school setting)
  b. document relevant details of academic, behavioral, social, and emotional functioning
  c. obtain information regarding home and community

☐ _Review of School Records and Previous Teachers' Reports_
PURPOSE:
  a. provide prior academic evidence of type, degree, and duration of child's ADD characteristics
  b. provide information about impact upon child's academic performance and social relations with peers and teachers

☐ _Relevant Medical Information from Child's Physician_ (to the extent such information exists)
PURPOSE:
  a. obtain history of any physical illnesses or injuries that may be associated with chronic or transient inattention or impulsivity
  b. obtain pertinent information about child's ADD characteristics
  c. obtain information about any medical therapies used or in use.

FOR CONSIDERATION
When rating scales demonstrate significant problems with attention absent impulsivity and hyperactivity, consider UADD. (DuPaul, 1992)

Rating Scales

To date, child behavior rating scales are the best available tools to determine presence of ADD characteristics and severity. A drawback is that scales are subject to bias. When differences are noted between ratings of parents and, teachers, more credence is generally given to teachers ratings since school is a more problematic setting for these children, and teachers have greater exposure to children within a specific age range. (DuPaul, 1992). Items on scales can be used in interviews to structure questions about ADD-related behaviors. (interview with Dr. Reeve, 1992)

Numerous rating scales exist. For a thorough review of rating scales and psychoeducational testing instruments, see _Attention Deficit Hyperactivity Disorder,_ Barkley, 1990 or _Managing Attention Disorders in Children,_ Goldstein & Goldstein, 1990. As with all psychoeducational tests and measures, rating scales have a range of error. School personnel should establish a range of error to operationalize the determination of "marked degree" — disproportionate for child's age. Rating scales used should have satisfactory normative information broadly representative of the child's chronological and mental age group.

PURPOSE:
  • determine presence of ADD symptoms
  • determine competing diagnoses information
  • determine degree of severity

RECOMMENDATIONS:
1. to look for competing diagnoses and ADD specific information, begin with a broad function scale. For example:
   • Child Behavior Check List, Teacher Report Form and Parent Report Form, by Achenbach & Edelbrock
   • Conners Parent Rating Scale & Conners Teacher Rating Scale Original Form, by Connors
   • Revised Behavior Problems Checklist, by Quay & Peterson
2. To measure ADD-related symptoms and severity, use scales specific to ADD. Data gathered here is also useful for Tier Two. For example:
   • ADHD Rating Scale for Parents or Teachers, by DuPaul (1990)
   • Home Situations Questionnaire, Revised, by DuPaul & Barkley (1990)
   • School Situations Questionnaire, Revised, by DuPaul & Barkley (1990)
   • Academic Performance Rating Scale, by DuPaul, Rapport & Perriello (1990) (also useful for determining adverse affect on academic performance)

TIER TWO
Determining Adverse Affect on Performance

Classroom Observation

PURPOSE: To focus on specific characteristics of ADD during individually performed assignments completed by child independent of teacher and during lectures.

☐ Record behaviors using direct and systematic observation 20–30 minutes on several different days at different times in 15–20 second intervals.

☐ Behaviors to record: off-task, fidgeting (repetitive, purposeless task irrelevant activity), out of seat (leaving chair without permission), vocalizing (any vocal noises or speech made during work periods), playing with objects (manipulative contact with objects unrelated to assigned activity).

☐ Use recorded observations to calculate percentage of occurrence for each behavioral category.
  • Instrument useful for recording observations: Restricted Academic Situation Coding Sheet, by Barkley and Crew.

FOR CONSIDERATON

By doing a comparison with peers, assessor is ensured that the child is compared to typical children within age or peer group. Such comparisons also control for confounding factors that cannot be taken into account in any set of national or regional norms, e.g., physical class structure, class size, teacher skill.

Academic Productivity

• *Evaluate with respect to child's intellectual ability* •

☐ Obtain I.Q. score to establish baseline of capability.

☐ Obtain estimate of child's work productivity and accuracy in relation to non-disabled peers and child's ability.

☐ Calculate percentage of work completed and percentage completed correctly during written assignments over 2 week period.

☐ Consider data in relation to teacher reports from Academic Performance Rating Scale.

Psychoeducational Tests

While not definitive or diagnostic of ADD, they can be adapted to provide information about the core features and how those interfere with task performance. They are also useful to establish coexistence of learning disabilities.

FOR CONSIDERATION

Due to structure and novelty of such tasks, expect better performance under one-to-one testing conditions.

Measures of Attention

Remind assessor to think about attention as a multifaceted construct and to differentiate attentional problems from language processing problems.

☐ Continuous Performance Tasks, which come in various forms ranging from simple, homemade paper and pencil measures such as ones which consist of entire pages of numbers or letters with instructions like "circle every 5 which has a 9 just before it," to computers with rapidly changing visual displays such as used in the Gordon Diagnostic System (GDS) or the Test of Variables of Attention (TOVA).

☐ WISC III Coding & Symbol Search, Trails Test on Halstead-Reitan Neuropsychological Battery — useful for ruling out impulsivity and ruling in inattentive, passive, daydreamy pattern associated with ADD without disinhibited/hyperactive pattern, result not definitive but offer corroborative evidence. (interview with Barkley, 1992).

FOR CONSIDERATION

The assessment protocol recommended by PGARD is sufficient to determine presence of ADD behaviors and adverse affect on educational performance. Medical input is desirable, however, to rule out treatable medical conditions that might be associated with ADD. Secondly, medical input can provide advice about the use of and indication for pharmacological intervention. Schools can thereby avoid problems which may arise from making recommendations for medication therapy.

(interview with Barkley, 1992)

Section Five

Interventions:
Principles and Practices

Interventions: Principles and Practices

When thinking about what to do for a child with ADD, one point becomes glaringly obvious. Presently, there is no known cure. Rather, ADD is a condition that is managed. Treatment approaches are designed to minimize the effects of the disability's symptomatology. Notice the operative is on managing symptomatology and not altering the basic nature of the child. We cannot change these children, nor is such a goal desirable. We can, however, help them compensate for their ADD-related difficulties.

Perhaps through knowledge and effort we can even prevent this disability's most debilitating effect, the loss of self-esteem. These children receive substantial amounts of negative feedback, of disapproval. They suffer academic and behavioral difficulties. Over time they grow to feel defeated and helpless. Considering that success in life is determined by a person's motivation, belief in self, and confidence, the effects of untreated ADD can and often do command too high a price.

Ultimately, all interventions have one goal — *to build the child's sense of competence.* Each short-term success builds long-term confidence. The way to increase self-esteem is to build competence and boost confidence by designing interventions and utilizing strategies that enable the child to feel a sense of "I can do." These children are not the children who *can't* or *won't*. Children with ADD can and do. It's just that *can* and *do* come harder to them. We each have strengths and limitations. Strengths, in particular, need to be identified in these students. Their limitations often capture too much attention.

Many educators, as well as parents, feel frustrated when their interventions do not seem to work. In fact, some do not. More often, however, the frustration comes from the expectation that the intervention effort will produce a change in the basic nature of the child. Of course, when we come to realize and accept that ADD is a neurobiologically-based problem, we understand the futility of this expectation. Interventions seek to manage ADD-related difficulties to achieve some semblance of normalcy. When all supports are arbitrarily withdrawn, expect the academic and behavioral difficulties of the student with ADD to almost certainly increase, and perhaps revert to pre-intervention levels.

Many interventions used will be short-term steps taken to create a positive self-image built upon a sense of self-confidence. Failure to keep this goal in mind, however, will cause many children to view intervention efforts as "just a new way for me to be labelled as a bad kid." Interventions designed to control the child generally produce that impression. These types of interventions do not provide access. They limit potential.

A Total Management Approach

Since ADD affects the child at home, in school, and with peers, researchers and clinical practioners recommend a multi-modal interdisciplinary management approach comprised of the following components:

- Knowledge of the disorder and understanding of how it affects the child at home, in school, with peers.
- Parent training in behavioral management techniques.
- Appropriate educational program, including behavioral management techniques.
- Pharmacological intervention when medically required.
- Individual and family counseling when needed.

In suggesting multi-modal treatment as the best alternative to facilitate a positive outcome for these children, clinicians emphasize that ADD is not just a school problem, or a home problem, or the child's problem for that matter. The components of the multi-modal management approach require a collaborative effort between the parents, educators, physician, and the child.

Since this manual's focus is on ADD in the school environment, intervention sections are concerned predominantly with school-based interventions. However, practically every public school has pupils in attendance who take medication for ADD; hence following is a brief discussion about medical management.

Medical Management

A vast literature exists on the use of medication therapy for children with ADD. The CH.A.D.D. Guide to Medical Management, reprinted in the appendix, reviews what types of medications are used and why.

Stimulant medications are the most widely used drugs for the management of behavioral symptoms in these children. Methylphenidate (Ritalin) is the most commonly prescribed drug. Research studies demonstrate that psychostimulant medications can have a strong, positive effect for a high percentage (70% or more) of children with ADD in that they decrease impulsivity and activity, and in some way narrow the range of attention, thus increasing perseverance. They also decrease aggression in some children. (interview with Swanson, 1992)

Unfortunately, stimulant medication is often used as a "silver bullet" rather than as one small part of a total management program. According to PGARD President James Swanson who also directs one the U.S. Education Department's ADD Centers, these medications do not necessarily improve learning. "Avoid the trap of thinking medication is effective because the child is quiet and still," he cautions. When evaluating medication efficacy, he recommends focusing on whether the child is able to grasp new material quicker, and not the effects it has on the adults in the child's life.

"Schools do not want to be in the business of prescribing medication, or being dependent on it," Dr. Swanson advises. To avoid the trap of practicing medicine without a license, schools can handle this delicate matter by providing parents with literature about the total treatment approach, recommending participation in an ADD parent support group, and/or recommending they consult their child's physician.

School (or parent) dependence on medication as the sole course of treatment is not recommended. Furthermore, dependence on medication as the most effective intervention may prove to be quite unreliable. According to Dr. Swanson, an interpretation of the exisiting body of literature suggests that 30% of the children stop taking medication within 2 years, and 60% within 3 years. Reasons for the discontinuance are speculative. Nonetheless, the implications of over-reliance are clear. Perhaps the use of medication is best viewed as a window of opportunity wherein educators focus on teaching organizational and learning strategies. Of course, such approaches should be used regardless of whether or not a child is on medication, but the child may be more available to learn these skills during the period when taking medication.

Some points to consider when a child takes medication during school are:

• Handle sensitively and discreetly. Avoid telling the child in front of the class or over the PA system that it's time to see the nurse, or worse, take his/her pill.

• Make sure the medication is dispensed as prescribed. Some leeway in time is permissible. For instance, the child does not have to be pulled out of an assembly or other rewarding activity to take medication at that very minute. The prescribing physician should provide a time range rather than a specific dosing time.

• Avoid giving too much credit or blame for the child's behavior to medication.

Like anybody else, the child will still have good and bad days. When problems arise, do not ask, "Did you take your pill this morning?"

• Monitor side effects. Communicate with parent or physician. Enlist the services of the school nurse or psychologist for evaluating effect as well as dosage.

Continuum of Services

Given that no two children with ADD are exactly alike, still the question arises, "What sorts of programs and interventions make sense for children with these types of problems?" Schools must obviously provide a continuum of services to meet individual needs. The following recommendations were made by the Professional Group for Attention and Related Disorders (PGARD) and the Virginia Department of Education Task Force on ADD.

Approximately 50% of children with ADD can be served within the regular education program if teachers are trained to recognize these students' special needs, and if appropriate modifications in the regular classroom setting are provided. Such modifications may include: curriculum adjustments, alterations to classroom organization and management, teaching techniques including the use of behavioral management strategies, and increased parent/teacher communication and collaboration.

In addition to these modifications, the other estimated 50% of children with ADD will require some degree of special education and related services. Of this 50%, approximately 35%-40% will primarily be served in the regular education classroom through combined services likely to include the addition of support personnel, and supplementary resources or resource pull-out programs. Support personnel are likely to act as case managers and consultants to regular education teachers to design, implement, and monitor special programs, for example:

• incorporating specific organizational techniques,

• daily interaction with child,

• frequent communication with parents,

• implementing special training and behavior modification techniques, including token reinforcement system to increase salience, timing, and consistency of behavioral consequences; daily report cards to provide potent positive consequences for performance; training self-monitoring and self-evaluation techniques for use in natural environment,

• coordinating efforts and reports between multiple teachers.

The most severely affected (assumed to be 10%-15%,) may require self-contained classrooms. Co-morbidity (the presence of other disorders) is likely to be a confounding factor with these children. When designing programs, consideration must be given to meeting all the child's educational needs, not just the ADD-related difficulties, or those related to the other disabilities but not ADD. Furthermore, as noted by the Virginia Department of Education Task Force Report on ADD, social skills deficits may be as debilitating to the function of these children as academic deficiences. Thus, if the student is doing well academically, but has significant difficulties with behavior and peer relations, assistance is both warranted and required.

Selecting Teachers

Psychology has long embraced the notion that people, environments, and individuals are either suited to each other (good matches), or they are not (poor matches). Most public school environments are dictated by variables which can rarely be changed to suit children with ADD. Class size, demands for sustained attention, and selection of curriculum reflect but a few such variables. Thus, we can assume at the outset that school environments are generally poor matches for the characteristics of ADD.

Yet, through anecdotal reports, we frequently hear that school success for children with ADD varies from year to year, class to class, and teacher to teacher. The teacher is most commonly cited as the reason for the positive or negative school experience. While much speculation exists about why some teachers appear to be better suited to teach students with ADD, Ross Greene,

Ph.D., Assistant Professor of Psychiatry and Pediatrics at the University of Massachusetts Medical Center is presently conducting research in an attempt to empirically determine which teacher characteristics are associated with successful school outcomes for students with ADD. "We are borrowing from studies related to both successful teaching of difficult students and successful parenting to try and extrapolate variables from these literatures that may be important in teaching students with ADD," he explains.

From the work of researchers on disability such as Jere Brophy, Hill Walker, James Kaufmann, Kathleen Wong, John Lloyd, and Barbara Larrivee, Dr. Greene cites the following list of teacher characteristics as likely indicators of positive educational outcomes for students with emotional and behavioral problems:

1. positive academic expectations
2. frequent monitoring and checking of student work
3. clarity (e.g., clear directions, standards, expectations)
4. flexibility (adapts as necessary, e.g., to modifications needed by certain students, schedule changes)
5. fairness (lack of favoritism)
6. active involvement with students (remains actively involved with students as they work)
7. responsiveness (attention to students' responses and comments)
8. warmth (good relationship with students, receptive to students' approaches)
9. patience
10. humor
11. structure (highly structured, predictable lessons)
12. consistency (sets and maintains contingencies)
13. firmness
14. knowledge of different types of behavioral interventions
15. positive attitude toward mainstreaming
16. knowledge and/or willingness to learn about working with students with emotional or behavioral problems and exceptional children in general

17. willingness to work with a special education teacher (e.g., share information regarding student's progress, seek assistance when needed, participate in meetings or conferences involving students)
18. high perception of self-efficacy (perceives self as competent teacher)
19. high sense of involvement (professional responsibility)
20. high professional job satisfaction

"All of these characteristics seem logically related to successful outcomes for students with ADD because they have to do with attitudes and beliefs, teaching and behavior management practices, knowledge of disability, and other components we suspect are related to a teacher's success with difficult students," notes Dr. Greene. These data also imply that students with ADD need teachers who have these attributes, because such teachers are able and willing to make adaptations to the environment that provide access for these students.

Food For Thought

TAKING CHARGE

Since the vast majority of children with ADD will spend the greatest portion of their time within regular education settings, teachers must have a realistic sense about their involvement. ADD-related difficulties pervade all subject areas all day long. "Teachers need to keep a positive action focus and avoid dangerous stances that blame the child, the parent, or themselves," notes Dr. Lauren Braswell, co-investigator of the National Institute of Mental Health funded Minnesota Competence Enhancement Program.

FAIR VERSUS EQUAL

Some teachers seem reluctant to make modifications and adaptations for children with ADD because they view that as unfair to other students. Executive Director of the Riverview School, Rick Lavoie, a noted special educator and lecturer observes, however, that fair does not mean equal. It does not mean that we do exactly the same for all children. For example, children with vision

problems are allowed to wear glasses. "These children with ADD have difficulty controlling attentional processes and behavior without help," explains Dr. Reeve, who adds, "In order for them to learn and behave better, they need to experience a high rate of success. They need people to respond favorably to them much more often than unfavorably; perhaps 80%-90% positive is an appropriate goal for responding."

RETENTION

Retention is seldom if ever a solution for these children. In the primary grades, the decision to retain a child is often based on the supposition that "the child just needs to mature." ADD is not a disorder of maturity. Considering retention on the grounds of immaturity may in fact be a tip-off to teachers and administrators to evaluate the child for suspected ADD.

In Practice

Numerous types and levels of interventions exist which enable the student with ADD to experience success academically, behaviorally, and socially. The challenge lies in using the information we know to create an environment that brings out the best in these students. Understandably, teachers sometimes resist putting forth the special effort required to utilize these techniques, but an important point to note is that the effort benefits all the students, not just those with ADD.

Borrowing From Instructional Theory

Instruction theory principles have major implications for teaching children with ADD. Those in the field of reading have long understood that in order to learn, children need to be experiencing success. Children are said to be appropriately placed in a reading level when they can read 90% of the words correctly. If they read fewer than 75%, they are said to be at the frustration level. At this level they do not benefit from the material. This notion has also been applied to other instructional materials in curriculum based assessments. Children are considered on grade level when they learn between 80%-90% of the material taught. (interview with Reeve, 1992) "Children with ADD need to experience that 80%-90% level of success, academically and behaviorally," says Dr. Reeve. Clearly, we cannot revise the neurobiological make-up of children with ADD. Instead, we must focus on changing attitudes and expectations, the classroom environment, and the curricula.

Matching Intervention Types

Many problems with intervention designs can be prevented by looking at the child's developmental level and anticipating needs. Dr. Reeve notes that the Piagetian developmental framework is useful for designing an overall template of the types of approaches used.

The following examples are his explanation of how this can be done. Preschool-kindergarten children are egocentric and very much driven by their impulses. They cannot step outside of self to evaluate their behavior. Trying to teach learning strategies is ineffective. Behavioral approaches, teaching routines, and manipulating the environment tend to have far more success at this stage.

Elementary school children begin to move outside of self and make evaluations. Children with ADD are delayed in

this process. Teaching organizational methods and routines while continuing behavioral approaches and environmental manipulations are most effective with these children.

Adolescent children are more reflective and cognitively able to deal with abstractions — the what ifs. They can think more objectively about themselves in relation to the world. They benefit from meta-cognitive kinds of strategies which help them to know how they think and learn. Teaching learning strategies and self-monitoring techniques work best with these young adults.

Notes on Practice

The strategies, techniques, and suggestions contained herein represent a sampling of educational practice to date. Educators should be advised that the research on what makes an optimal educational program for children with ADD is still somewhat preliminary. Presently there is ample knowledge about how to manipulate the classroom environment to make it more conducive to children with ADD-related characteristics. There is also good knowledge about how to manage the children's ADD-related behavioral difficulties. For example, we know positive feedback develops a sense of competence so critical for self-esteem! We also know failure to use these available methods renders the like-

---

FOR CONSIDERATION

Specific interventions and techniques must clearly be chosen with consideration for each child's unique needs, the teacher's style, and a host of other variables that come with living in the real world. As you try suggestions, do not be discouraged if you do not meet with immediate success, or even if the idea bombs. A large part of managing ADD involves trying until you find what works.

---

ly outcome for children with ADD dismal.

In all candor, the best classroom practices probably have yet to be developed. Federal dollars are only now beginning to make their way into the field of education for specific ADD-related activities. CH.A.D.D. sincerely hopes this section of the *Educators Manual* will need revision in the near future as educators create better programs for children with ADD. For now the following strategies and techniques have shown a good degree of effectiveness based upon research available to date.

Ingredients For Improving Performance

Most children with ADD require some necessary interventions in the environment and curricula to improve academic and behavioral performance. Some of the following interventions fall under the rubric of "good teaching" suggesting application to all students. They may well be, but, *when these interventions are not used for students with ADD these children have a very difficult time meeting academic and behavioral expectations.*

The suggestions on the next pages fall under three major categories: (A) behavior management, (B) classroom

organization and management, and (C) modified curriculum. Within each of these categories are suggested activities which may involve the provision of a reward. For convenience, the following reward menu is presented.

REWARD MENU

ACTIVITY REWARDS

Earning special privileges such as choosing the class's recess activity, being first in line, serving as a messenger or disc jockey during a music period, computer/video games, free homework night, free time, phone call from or lunch with the teacher, lunch or breakfast with the principal, auc-

tion for desirable classroom item — such as flannel story board or bulletin board pictures

---

TANGIBLE REWARDS

Candy, gum, popcorn, miscellaneous small school supplies, stickers, paper clips, pencils, special certificates, coupons from local merchants, "Flying A" (used to change a grade or make up a missing grade).

GROUP/CLASS ACTIVITY

Earning extra recess or free time for music, art, or other activities of their choice, earning the privilege of a class-wide game, class parties with popcorn, pizza, gum, cookies, etc.

GUIDELINES and PRACTICES

Behavior Management

Behavior management strategies are designed to increase positive and appropriate behavior. Types of strategies range from paying positive attention to very formal behavior modification programs. The following section of this manual explains and illustrates formal behavior management systems and school-based programs. For now, the focus is on paying positive attention.

CATCH THE CHILD BEING GOOD AND DOING WELL

Paying positive attention may not always come naturally. When frustration is high, it may not come at all. Children with ADD require a high percentage of positives. Sometimes it is helpful to ask their input about what areas they feel are their strengths and then make a point of reinforcing them. Even though appropriate behavior is expected, praising its use will increase its frequency.

GUIDELINES

► Use frequent eye contact to get and keep the child's attention.

► Cultivate a safe, classroom atmosphere absent all ridicule.

► Act rather than react to behavior, thus resisting an adult's tendency to respond impulsively rather than think before taking action.

► Respond calmly when behavior is inappropriate. (Training ourselves to count to five first defuses harshness and guards against angry responses that show rejection to the child.)

► Use positive actions and commands that tell the child what is expected, instead of what is not. Use statements like "I want you to…" or commands that begin in the affirmative, such as "Put the pencil down, please."

PRACTICES

(The following suggestions were designed by the mentor teachers of the Los Angeles Unified School District (LAUSD) after participating in a conference on ADD presented by Lauren Braswell, Ph.D., through the University of Minnesota Department of Professional Development and Continuing Education. They have been shown to be successful when used with ADD students.

Unless otherwise designated, they appear to have use at all age and grade levels. As with any suggestion, individual need and circumstance must be taken into account. Additional LAUSD suggestions and practices are listed throughout this section.)

☐ CAUGHT BEING GOOD
Children are given "Caught Being Good" cards or "Blitz Bucks" for particularly positive behavior. When they have received 5 or 10 of the cards, they cash them in for prizes.

☐ SPELL-A-REWARD
A class-wide program (at the secondary level) involves awarding a letter to individuals who exhibit appropriate behavior for the class period. Enough individual letters have to be earned to spell out a predetermined rewarding activity, e.g., popcorn party, free time, no homework.

☐ PUT ON A HAPPY FACE
Maintain a class chart and award happy faces for appropriate behavior. For 5 happy faces, the child can get something from the reward jar. For extra special behavior, the child can get a special trip to the jar.

☐ ALL ON TIME RAFFLE
On the secondary level, for each two-week period, students with all the materials in on-time, and without tardies or absences, receive a raffle ticket which goes into a pool for a drawing.

☐ BLOW BUBBLES
Whenever the class is behaving appropriately, put pennies into a jar. When 100 pennies are accumulated, the class has a bubble gum party.

☐ WHIZ KID
Give out "Whiz Kid" cards to recognize students showing significant improvement in specific areas, either academic or behavioral.

☐ MOBILE MOTIVATION
On the primary level, place mobiles over each worktable. When the children at a particular table display good behavior, they earn an object to place on their mobile. The tables compete to see who will be first to complete their mobile.

☐ TICKET TICKLER
Give tickets to students for completed work, appropriate behavior, etc. These tickets are used in a drawing that occurs daily, weekly, or biweekly.

A POSITIVE ATTITUDE BAROMETER

The following activity, suggested by Dr. Reeve, is designed to help teachers assess the rate at which they make positive comments and then to improve positive attending:

☐ Wear something with pockets.
   Place 20 chips in the right hand pocket. During a 1 hour time period, each time a positive comment is made to a student, move a chip to the left hand pocket. How did you do?

☐ Repeat the exercise. This time the goal is to move all 20 chips from the right to the left hand pocket.

☐ Repeat the exercise, but this time only move a chip after making a positive comment to the student with ADD. How many did you move? (Obviously, moving all 20 in 1 hour might be overdoing it a bit and may even appear contrived to this student.) Praise needs to be valid. Providing positive attention must become a habit.

Classroom Organization And Management

These children often tend to miss the neutral information in a structure. Their environment needs to be highly ordered and predictable. Rules and expectations must be clear.

GUIDELINES

Classroom organization:

▶ Four walls and a door.

▶ Display classroom rules/prompts.

▶ Post daily schedule and homework assignments in the same place.

▶ Call attention to any changes in the schedule.

▶ Set aside specific periods for specific tasks.

▶ Ease transitions between classes and activities by providing clear directions, and cues such as 5 minute warnings prior to the transition.

▶ Provide a quiet work area used at student's request (not to be confused with a place to punish).

▶ Seat away from auditory distractors.

▶ Seat next to positive peer models.

Classroom management:

▶ Plan academic subjects for morning hours.

▶ Provide regularly scheduled and frequent breaks.

▶ Train students to recognize "time to begin work" cues, e.g., teacher closes door, teacher stands and faces class.

▶ Seat close to teacher, but with rest of class.

▶ Use various attention-getting devices, e.g., secret signals, finger snaps, color-coded cards.

PRACTICES

(Suggested by LAUSD personnel)

☐ INSTRUCTIONAL AIDE
Make the fidgety child the instructional aide and have him/her teach a follow-up lesson to the class, or serve as a tutor to another child. Students with ADD respond well to tutoring children from lower grades.

☐ POSITIVE RESPONSES
Teach students to use encouraging and reinforcing comments with each other to acknowledge good work products and/or good effort.

☐ THE COLOR OF RULES
In primary grades, four or five key rules are color-coded and written on placards which are posted around the room. When a student is having difficulty with a particular rule, the teacher addresses this by saying, "Suzie, red." Rules have to be brief and stated in positive terms, e.g. "Follow directions," "Listen," "Keep Your Space," etc.

☐ THE BIG CHILL-OUT
Several teachers suggest training the class to relax via listening to music or other relaxation methods. On days when students seem headed for behavioral difficulties or when all are overexcited, the teacher uses the relaxation methods to prevent development of more serious difficulties.

Modifying Curriculum

Many students with ADD will need reductions in the amount of work assigned and more time to complete assignments. (See section two for rationale and specific guidelines for structuring tasks.) In general, these children will need a more stimulating, active curriculum.

GUIDELINES

▶ Provide high interest, high motivation tasks.

▶ Use mixture of high and low interest tasks, e.g., follow lecture with hands-on activity.

▶ Provide computer learning materials.

▶ Simplify and heighten visual presentations by using clearly printed, uncluttered work sheets. Color emphasize key elements or work phrases, use directional arrows, green and red start-stop indicators, color blocking.

▶ Provide programmed materials requiring correction before proceeding which thereby structure approach to task.

▶ Include organizational and study skills as part of the curriculum (see section three).

▶ Use visual references for auditory instruction.

▶ Alternate activities to eliminate desk fatigue.

▶ Use computers to teach writing skills.

PRACTICES

(Suggested by the LAUSD personnel)

To encourage team work:

□ LEARNING PARTNERS
Create learning partnerships in which a more calm/or advanced student is paired with the child with ADD to help him/her learn new concepts or practice the use or previously introduced skills. Some teachers suggest that, on occasion, make team members' grades on a particular worksheet, assignment, or test dependent upon one another to ensure that partners take study efforts seriously.

□ GROUP MIXERS
With students in 4th grade or above, have students work in cooperative mixed ability groups with group reward reinforcement system and individual rewards. This system includes extra rewards when the full group meets agreed upon standards. This system can be used to achieve not only academic content goals, but also social skills and behavioral compliance expectations.

□ SURE SUCCESS
To combat student demoralization, try to give each student at least one task each day that he or she can do successfully, e.g. explaining something to somebody else, assisting another student on the playground.

To encourage active student participation:

□ PLAY ACT
Use role-playing or dramatic play to illustrate certain concepts (e.g. over, under, between) or contents (social studies material, historical events).

□ SIGN SPELLING
Use sign language to teach spelling. Teachers recommend putting up a poster of sign language.

□ SRA
A number of teachers recommended the SRA Corrective Reading System. This system allows children to respond throughout a teacher directed lesson. Students get points that are assigned to the student group for appropriate responding which they exchange for a small treat or reward.

□ BOARD WORK
Having children work at the board increases level of involvement and more children can participate if some are designated workers and others are checkers.

□ PLAYING SIDES
Designate half the class "A's" and half as "B's". The teacher tells the B's they don't have to listen and teaches a new concept to the A's. Then the A's are told to teach the B's. Alternate which group gets to play the role of instructor.

□ HANDS ON
• Cut apart sentences and then have students arrange parts on a slant or felt board to learn about sentence structure.

• Have students snap or clap out the answer to a math problem.

□ KEEPING ACTIVE IN MIND
Invite active responses by encouraging all students to respond to teacher's questions "in mind" first, and then having one or more students respond in overt manner. (This method has added benefit of encouraging reflective responding.) Variations for overt

responses include:

- have students stand or sit to indicate their response

- use individual chalk boards to write down and display answers

- hold up cards to answer questions

- indicate a "yes" answer with thumbs up; a "no" with thumbs down

- use four corners of the classroom to indicate true, false, don't know, or no answer and then have students listen to question and move to, point to, or face the corner that indicates their response

- have students act out the actions of characters in stories that are being read aloud

- have students march, sing, dance, or speak a key concept while the class chants and follows the leader in a slow-moving snake dance around the room

- use learning games, such as Simon Says,

- use chain method of creating stories to get input from all students

"Do not send unfinished classwork home. Classwork is within a teacher's jurisdiction and not the parents'. If classwork is incomplete, then it is corrected by changing its management at school, and not by dumping it into the home."

Dr. Barkley

The guidelines and practices provide the motivation, involvement and structure so desperately needed by children with ADD. They make the classroom environment accessible.

Section Six

Behavioral Interventions

Behavioral Interventions

Getting "BAC" To Basics

The intervention principles and practices put forth in the previous section are examples of how the regular program of instruction can be modified to assist these children. Clearly, adding ingenuity and creativity to the basic guidelines make the possibilities limitless.

Yet, even with such strategies and techniques, many children with ADD are so significantly impaired that such general guidelines will not be enough to improve their academic and behavioral performance commensurate with their ability and with classroom expectations. The issue confronting most teachers is how to best respond to unacceptable behavior when nothing they do seems to work.

Designing Interventions

Knowing that a child is inattentive, impulsive, or hyperactive does not really provide enough information about the various behaviors the child exhibits or what to do about them.

Behavioral theory suggests that behaviors are preceded by antecedents and followed by consequences. Antecedents (that which come before) set the stage for the behavior to occur. Consequences (that which follow) provide either the reward or the punishment. Rewards increase the likelihood of behaviors recurring. Punishment decreases the likelihood of behaviors recurring. This section title, *Getting "BAC" to Basics,* is a play on an often-missed point about behavioral difficulties, specifically that incidents have three components: behaviors (B), antecedents (A), and consequences (C). Basic problem-solving requires identifying the B, A, and C in each incident.

Effective interventions are geared toward eliminating the cause of behaviors. According to Dr. Zentall, "The only way to find the cause of a behavior is to analyze the antecedents and consequences. Then you formulate a hypothesis and make a change." She also considers it important to find what the child is working for (the consequences), because then you can give that consequence to the student, only on your terms, not his/hers. Generally, the child is working to get out of or away from something, or to get something.

FOR CONSIDERATION

The term "behavior" is used here in the global sense. Behavior refers to more than disruption. Approach to task, task performance (accuracy as well as completion) are all behavioral in nature.

The answer to the question, "What do I do when I see X behavior? when nothing I do seems to work?" is *analyze.* Otherwise, the old belief system that the child is willfully noncompliant, or just not trying, creeps into the thinking and distorts action. In some cases, an analysis will require the help of support personnel, as will some of the interventions designed to alleviate the student's problems.

Functional Approach

Following are guidelines for analyzing problematic behaviors which educators can use to facilitate the creation of effective interventions designed for individual student/teacher needs.

GUIDELINES

☐ Describe the problem behavior in objective, nonjudgmental terms.

☐ Identify the antecedents (prompts or cues that seem to set the occasion for the behavior).

☐ Identify the consequences (what happens) and note how after they follow the problem behavior and on what schedule.

☐ Analyze how antecedents and consequences affect behavior.

☐ Design interventions that change antecedents and/or reinforcers. (Notice you don't change behavior. You change the cause, the payoff, or both. Behavior then changes as a result.)

☐ Evaluate effectiveness of interventions and make necessary adjustments.

To utilize this functional analysis approach, Dr. Zentall recommends that describing the problem and identifying the antecedents and consequences be done in a diary format (or a set of notes), with the teacher writing down over a 2–4 week period all problematic incidents and how s/he typically responds to those incidents. The diary allows the teacher to identify problem settings and the probable consequences. Using this journal format also has the advantage of enabling educators to identify a student's behavioral patterns and thereby design interventions aimed at the student's central issues. Otherwise, the teacher is apt to become mired in addressing specific incidents of behavior which can be very tedious, and perhaps even deleterious. The use of special education personnel working in conjunction with the teacher may be helpful in defining the pattern(s) of the behavior(s) and designing interventions.

EXAMPLE:
FUNCTIONAL ANALYSIS
Case #1

Description:

John, a third grade student, is often noncompliant and does not begin tasks when asked. During a two-week observation period, John did the following and often on a daily basis.

John sharpened his pencil three times before sitting down and working. John fell out of his chair when given an assignment with 50 problems. He pretended to be a clown. The class laughed. After reading group, on the way back to his seat for independent work. John tripped Sally. He was sent to the corner of the room.

Identifying Antecedents
and Consequences:

In John's case, you'll notice most behavioral difficulties occur at the beginning of tasks. Dr. Zentall suggests that there is something about the tasks that the child is attempting to avoid. Either they are too long, or too difficult, or lack interest. To avoid the tasks, the child misbehaves and gets social attention in return. His peers laugh. His teacher sends him to the back of the room. He has avoided the work momentarily.

Effectively Reponding To This
Behavioral Pattern Requires:

Analyzing how antecedents and consequences affect behavior by asking: Does he avoid all tasks? Are there specific tasks he likes? How can the tasks be made more like those he enjoys? Is the task too long? Too Difficult? Lacking in novelty? What is John getting? He is getting out of doing work and social attention.

Designing Interventions
- ► Short-term for task avoidance:
- Make the tasks more like the tasks he enjoys or change the reinforcers. For example, tell John that if he gets to reading group before anyone else, he gets to pass out the materials.

- ► Long-term for task avoidance:
- Teach alternative ways to avoid tasks without being behaviorally disruptive, e.g., encourage the child to identify when a task is too hard, or if the print is too small, and to say so quietly.

Changing Social Reinforcers:

Understanding in this case that the child is working for and receiving social attention enables the teacher to use this very powerful reward as part of the learning task and a subsequent consequence. The teacher could use peer tutoring for the learning portion of the task. A social consequence would be telling the student that if the task is completed in the required time, he can wash the board with a friend.

Case #2

Description:

Sally is a middle school or senior high student who never gets from class A to class B on time. Often she doesn't have the materials necessary for the next class. Her tardiness interferes with the class routine. Sally often misses class directions because she is busy trying to make up for lost time. The class has already started working, while she is looking for yesterday's homework, which she ultimately remembers was left in the locker.

Identifying The Antecedents
And Consequences:

The teacher observes Sally at the end of the period and in the hallway. Sally takes longer to put away her materials. After leaving class, she stops at her locker. She talks to just about everybody who passes. Then, realizing it is late, she rushes to the next class and forgets to get necessary materials, but Sally does get social time.

Effectively Responding To This
Student's Behavior Would Require:

Analyzing how antecedents and consequences affect behavior by asking: Why does Sally have trouble getting to class on time? The hallway presence of friends and absence of structure or supervision are the cues as they set the occasion for socializing. Because Sally takes longer to put materials away at the end of class her social time is jeopardized. In order to maintain social time, Sally overlooks the primary purpose for going to her locker.

The simple fact that it takes Sally longer to put away her materials could set off a chain reaction of academic and behavioral difficulties. By using a little

imagination, you can see how tardiness and unpreparedness would likely become antecedents for a whole series of behavioral incidents potentially resulting in Sally's academic failure and the development of disciplinary problems. The root cause of Sally's difficulty is easily managed. But, if the antecedent is not identified, the teacher(s) could spend much time and energy reacting and responding to the other behavioral difficulties which actually result from the antecedent.

Designing Interventions
- ► Short-term:

Structure the situation so there is no way Sally can be late to the next class. Have her begin to put away her materials a few minutes before the other students and then make a list of what is needed for the next class. Send Sally to her locker a few minutes before everybody else. Check the list. If Sally gets all the necessary materials, she is rewarded with a few minutes to talk to friends.

- ► Intermediate:

Reduce the amount of extra time allotted sequentially.

- ► Long-term:

Sally leaves at the same time as everyone else, gets all the materials needed, arrives to class B on time, and perhaps early enough to socialize before "time to begin work" cue is given.

Using the functional analysis approach, as with the development of any skill, may initially seem cumbersome. Once the skill is trained, however, this problem-solving process moves quickly. In fact, it may actually save time, since behavioral incidents tend to be variations of a basic theme. Interventions are more likely to be positive and successful because they are designed to eliminate the cause of the behavior and not the result of it.

ROUTINES AS ANTECEDENTS

Routines alleviate any situation that requires a standard response not involving thought. Children with ADD do not readily develop routines. Consequently, they tend to be disorganized. In fact, Dr. Zentall has found the lack of routines to be an antecedent for many behaviors. For example, work is often not handed in when completed, or doesn't make it to home and back, or is shoved into a desk, etc., because the child does not have a routine for what happens in these situations. She advises figuring out those places where the child could be using routines to alleviate problems. This might include teaching a routine for what happens when tasks are completed. For example, cue the child two minutes before the bell rings to proceed to the end of task routine. Completed work goes in X folder on the teacher's desk or a specific place in the child's desk. Uncompleted work goes in the homework folder.

FOR CONSIDERATION

Routines need to be brief and uncomplicated. Allowing the child to select components of the various routines helps the child to be committed to their use.

Routines can also be useful in social situations. Children with ADD typically barge into group situations. This behavior often results in rejection. Dr. Zentall recommends training such students to follow a simple routine for entering groups, e.g., first standing outside the group for two minutes to listen and watch, and then commenting about what someone said or did as a point of entry. They must be cautioned, however, that the use of the routine does not always result favorably.

Self-Monitoring Techniques

Researchers at the University of Minnesota are currently conducting a 22-school study to determine the effectiveness of cognitive/behavioral interventions for children with ADD. Within the realm of cognitive/behavioral interventions, according to team member Dr. Braswell, researchers have found success with the use of self-monitoring techniques. Though primarily used to monitor attention to task, these self-

monitoring strategies have also been applied to specific behaviors such as interrupting and blurting out in class. These techniques can be used by regular or special education teachers.

Self-monitoring of attention involves cueing the student so that the student can determine the extent to which s/he is on or off-task. This technique, which can be used with one child or an entire class, is recommended for second grade students and older. Usually such cueing is done by providing an audio tone in the form of a random beep, though a timer can be used, or the teacher can give the cue. Upon hearing the cue, the child makes a notation on a simple recording sheet denoting whether s/he was on or off-task. (Students with more severe ADD problems may require the use of a paraprofessional to provide cues and monitor recording, or the techniques may need to be taught in a pull-out program, and then introduced within the regular classroom setting.)

Dr. Braswell notes that self-monitoring of attention leads to improved use of independent study and work time. As with many interventions, the technique works *while in use,* but does not change or improve the student's ability to sustain attention. With older children, perhaps middle school and above, Dr. Braswell says the technique can be used for lecture as well as independent work. Younger children, however, would have a difficult time discriminating between on/off-task behavior during teacher led instruction.

In training teachers to use this technique, Dr. Braswell observes that most are reticent until they actually use the method. They then find that initially students listen for the tone rather than concentrate on their work, but that this effect dissipates quickly, and on-task performance improves. Dr. Braswell also encourages teachers to have the students calculate their own percentage of on/off-task behavior and tie some type of reward to on-task behavior, such as giving bonus points.

Self-monitoring can also be adapted to encourage children in the third grade or above not to interrupt or blurt out in class. One simple technique is to provide the child with a sheet that looks like a clock face. Each minute or five minutes (depending on the child) that the child

does not blurt out, s/he earn points. "A nice aspect to this use is that it keeps the focus on the positive alternative," explains Dr. Braswell.

Teachers tend to like self-monitoring techniques because they provide a sense of the child taking responsibility. Additionally, they provide steady feedback without being judgmental. (interview with Dr. Braswell, 1992)

Most self-monitoring techniques have their greatest effect when tied to some form of reward and accuracy check. Accuracy checks do not have to occur every time the technique is in use. When doing accuracy checks, the teacher uses the same tone cue as the students. When the tone beeps, the teacher looks at the child and records whether they were on/off-task. At the end of a 20–30 minute work period, the teacher then moves about the room and provides individual feedback to the students. Bonus points can then be given for accuracy, even in circumstances where the child was off-task. Here, the reward is for honesty. (interview with Dr. Brasell, 1992).

With older students, these techniques can be modified to have students rate the appropriateness of their overall behavior. In this modification, called "matching," the student's overall rating must agree with the independent rater (usually a para-professional). (interview with Dr. Braswell, 1992)

Traditional cognitive approaches, such as "stop and think" problem-solving methods, do not tend to be successful for students with ADD. In order to be somewhat effective, they must be used in environmental contexts where teachers and parents are modeling the same kinds of approaches. Dr. Braswell believes, however, that problem-solving strategies can be useful for anger arousal and certain chronic situations, like homework hassles. "If a child has a certain issue that is chronic, it's worth your time and the student's time to sit down and problem-solve for alternatives." she adds. Often problem-solving over chronic issues, e.g., getting papers from school to home and back to school, results in the creation of a routine.

For students who exhibit difficulties controlling their attentional processes and impulsivity, logic suggests that teaching them to stop and think makes great sense. Yet, as Dr. Braswell explains,

"Stop and think" approaches may have their greatest effect on the adults in the child's life. When the adults stop and think, they become less reactive. "This method provides an alternative to the adults. They do not have to be lost in that old cycle of anger," notes Dr. Braswell.

if these students could pick up these approaches based on natural contigencies, that would have happened.

Principles of Behavior Management

The following information on behavioral principles and how to apply them for use with ADD students is quoted from *The ADD Hyperactivity Handbook for Schools,* by Harvey Parker, Ph.D., Impact Publication, 1992. (Used with author's permission.)

Teachers have applied behavior modification principles in classrooms for many years. Behavior modification assumes that teachers can increase, decrease, or eliminate specific behaviors of their students by manipulating responses which follow those behaviors.

Three types of responses can affect behavior:

- positive reinforcement,
- negative reinforcement,
- and punishment or response-cost.

Positive reinforcement involves the administration of a pleasurable or rewarding response to the student following the demonstration of a specific behavior. Positive reinforcers increase the likelihood of a behavior recurring. By using positive reinforcement to strengthen an appropriate behavior we can simultaneously weaken another, incompatible, inappropriate behavior. For example, a

teacher will strengthen in-seat behavior by praising a student for sitting at his desk, while at the same time weakening out-of-seat behavior since the two behaviors are incompatible.

Negative reinforcement removes an aversive or uncomfortable event following the demonstration of a specific behavior. Negative reinforcers also increase the likelihood of a behavior recurring.

Punishment, or response-cost, involves the presentation of an aversive or uncomfortable consequence to the student or the removal of the student from a positive situation following the demonstration of a specific behavior. Punishment, or response-cost, decreases the likelihood of a behavior recurring.

Applying principles of positive reinforcement, negative reinforcement, and punishment properly requires the teacher to evaluate what is rewarding and what is not rewarding to the individual student. Students differ greatly in their response to consequences. For example, social praise may be rewarding to some students, but embarrassing to others, just as punishments may vary in their effectiveness from student to student. Determining how rewarding or punishing a consequence is for a student can be accomplished by questioning the student or by applying such consequences and observing the effects on the student's behavior.

How To Use Behavioral Principles For Students With ADD

1. Select a specific behavior you want to increase.

2. Record each time the behavior occurs over a given period of time. For example, how often the student starts a task within two minutes after the task is given.

3. Analyze the antecedents and consequences.

4. If your goal is to improve the frequency of a targeted behavior, then select a reinforcer which you think the student prefers. Oftentimes good reinforcers can be determined by asking the student what they would like or by watching to see their preferred interests. Built-in reinforcers are common in the classroom, for in

stance, attention and praise, awarding of jobs, offering of free time, reduction in amount of work required, etc.

5. When initially teaching a new behavior, it is important to present positive reinforcements immediately and continuously. This occurs by immediately providing reinforcement every time the behavior occurs. At first the child may not demonstrate the target behavior. In that case, it would be necessary to reinforce behaviors approximating the target behavior. This is called shaping behavior. For instance, a student who does not complete independent assignments might never obtain a reinforcement for completed work, but this student could be reinforced for doing a certain amount and then reinforced again for doing more, and so on until this student's behavior was shaped to complete entire assignments.

6. If positive reinforcement is not effective in improving a behavior, even after several different reinforcers have been tried, then the teacher might need to use negative reinforcement or punishment to change behavior. It is usually best, however, to give the positive reinforcement program a good chance to work before applying negative methods.

Negative reinforcement allows the child to avoid an aversive consequence by behaving in a specific way. In using negative reinforcement, the student should be told what to do to avoid the aversive consequence. If the student does not do what is asked, provide the consequence in a firm, business-like way without emotion, lectures, or long-winded explanations to the student.

Punishment involves the removal of the student from having a positive experience or the application of an aversive consequence. The aversive consequence or punishment is presented after the inappropriate behavior is demonstrated with the expectation that the behavior will decrease after it is punished. When using punishment it is important to make sure that the consequence delivered to the student is indeed aversive. For instance, teacher attention, even negative teacher attention, may be reinforcing to the student. Getting in trouble may be amusing to the student, may create popularity with other students, and may get the student out of being in class or out of having to do unpleasant work.

While a consequence may seem aversive to the teacher, it may not be negative to the student. Therefore, it will not carry the weight of punishment and will not result in a decline in inappropriate behavior. The teacher needs to find the right punishment for the behavior and for the child. Overpunishing or delivering punishments in an emotionally harsh manner discourages, angers, and demoralizes students, and can produce more negative than positive effects. Punishment, when used, should be administered sparingly and judiciously.

In Summary

The invention principles, practices, problem-solving approaches, and most of the strategies explained in Section Five and in this section are useful for children with ADD at *all* grade levels. Educators are advised, however, that middle school and senior high students will respond better when they are actively engaged in the decision-making process. For example, when designing behavioral contracts, or when developing routines, allow the student to provide input and make choices. In doing so, ownership is transferred to the adolescent. Such ownership reduces the resistance which often accompanies the "it's being done to me" attitude many adolescents will adopt.

Two Model Programs

Following is an overview of two university-affiliated model programs which use a heavy behavior modification approach. The University of California, Irvine program, directed by James Swanson, Ph.D., has a model currently being used within regular education settings in conjunction with the Irvine Unified School District. Ron Kotkin, Ph.D. is coordinator of the school-based program in Irvine. The University of Massachusetts Medical Center research program, under the direction of Russel Barkley, Ph.D., is being conducted in conjunction with the Worcester Public Schools. Terri Shelton, Ph.D., is co-investigator. Preliminary results of both programs are promising. These program descriptions appeared in the Spring/Summer 1992 issue of CHADDER.

School-Based Interventions For ADD Students

Model Programs of the Child Development Center, University of California, Irvine

by

James M. Swanson, Ph.D.; Ron Kotkin, Ph.D.; Linda Pfiffner, Ph.D.; and Keith McBurnett, Ph.D. (reprinted from CHADDER, Spring/Summer 1992)

University of California, Irvine Child Development Center (UCI-CDC) psychologists, educators, and physicians have developed three models for school-based intervention with ADD students in elementary school:

(1) the parallel teaching model
(2) the paraprofessional teaching model
(3) the multicomponent model

These three model programs are designed for children with ADD with different degrees of educational impairment. The "parallel teaching" model alters the regular classroom to fit the needs of children who do not require special education and related services. The "paraprofessional teaching model provides additional resources in the regular classroom for students who require special education and related services. The multicomponent model establishes a self-contained classroom and a school-based clinical intervention program for children with ADD with severe educational impairments.

All three models are based on the assumption that the attentional and motivational problems of students with ADD are manifested continuously throughout the day and thus require interventions which are applied throughout the day while the child with ADD is in the school setting. The UCI-CDC uses general behavior modification principles and techniques in all three models.

1. The Parallel Teaching Model

Pfiffner led the development of a program at UCI-CDC to train teachers to use frequent and brief specialized interventions blended with their regular teaching styles. Teachers are trained to do two things in parallel: to conduct academic instruction, (i.e., to carry out a lesson plan), and to scan the room to provide redirection and reinforcement to the student with ADD in an average-size class.

The goal of parallel teaching is to increase frequency of teacher-child interaction by systematic applications of basic behavioral techniques: (a) positive reinforcement, i.e., the "catch the child being good" technique to encourage attentive on-task behavior, (b) prudent negatives, i.e., the "catch the child before getting bad" technique to avoid escalation of disruptive behaviors. To accomplish parallel teaching, training and practice is required to make these simple but powerful techniques become "second nature" to the teacher. Positive consequences, e.g., teacher attention, privileges, access to preferred activities, etc, must be used to shape and maintain attentive behavior and completion of academic work in students with ADD. Prudent negative consequences must be timed and delivered early in the typical sequences which usually escalate to classroom disruption and require severe negative consequences, e.g., time-out, detention, etc.

UCI-CDC evaluators of children with ADD are often informed by school personnel that "behavior modification in the regular classroom has been tried and does not work." In such cases, UCI-CDC staff rigorously review the way behavioral techniques were applied before accepting that this level of intervention has failed. Nonetheless, they expect that in about one-half of the ADD cases, the severity of educational symptoms are too great to be altered significantly by the regular classroom teacher alone. Effective interventions with children impaired to this extent require extra classroom staff, i.e., a classroom aide, to allow for an increase in the frequency and intensity in the delivery of positive and negative consequences in the regular classroom.

2. The Paraprofessional Model

In collaboration with the Irvine Unified School District (IUSD), the UCI-CDC staff developed this model program for moderately impaired students with ADD who could be well-served when provided supplementary services delivered in the regular classroom. Kotkin led the development of a UCI-CDC program to train teachers' aides (paraprofessionals) and regular classroom teachers to use specific techniques which are effective with students with ADD. The UCI-IUSD paraprofessional intervention model utilized three methods of intervention: (a) a skills remediation component, conducted in small groups in which the paraprofessional uses "coaching" and continuous reinforcement to shape new social skills and to develop language and cognitive behavior modification programs in the classroom; (b) a classroom performance component in which the paraprofessional works as a teacher's aide to facilitate the use of parallel teaching model and to help implement a token economy with frequent and consistent token reinforcers (points) and potent activity reinforcers which are necessary for these educationally impaired students; (c) a daily report component which replaces the intensive "point system" and allows the presence of the paraprofessional in the regular classroom to be reduced and eventually faded out over a 12 week period.

In the UCI-IUSD paraprofessional model, two half-time behavioral specialists (highly trained classroom aides) are assigned to a school of approximately 600 students. Based on current prevalence figures, it is expected that 10-12 of the school's students may have ADD with moderate impairment. Twice a week, in groups of four, these moderately impaired students with ADD attend a 30-45 minute skill training group in which continuous reinforcement is used to shape new social and cognitive skills which these children often lack. Over a 6 to 12 week period, these groups are used to cover a curriculum designed to develop and practice specific skills, (e.g. cooperation, communication, participation, validation, assertion without aggression, etc.) and rules, (e.g., raising hand to talk, staying seated, following directions to a "T", etc.). The paraprofessional who conducts the skill training group also returns to the classroom with the students to serve as the classroom aide. Initially, the extra classroom aide time may amount to 15 hours per week (3 hours per day for 5 days a week) for each classroom containing one or more of the students with ADD who are concurrently in the twice-a-week skill training group.

Later, if the paraprofessional program is effective, the extra classroom aide time is reduced to between 6 and 8 hours a week. After approximately 12 weeks, the behavioral specialist is completely withdrawn, and the regular classroom teacher alone maintains the classroom program by applying the parallel teaching model described above.

The group skill training alone does not have a significant impact on the academic performance or behavior of children with ADD in the regular classroom. Classroom effects are dependent upon the "trainer" (the paraprofessional behavioral specialist who leads the skills group) acting as a classroom aide to provide "reinforced practice" in the regular classroom. This seems to be essential to achieve generalization, and it also increases involvement and cooperation of the regular classroom teacher.

3. The Multicomponent Model

In ADD cases with severe educational impairment placement in a self-contained classroom may be required. Such cases are likely to have ADD plus co-existing SLD or SED. In collaboration with the Orange County Department of Education (OCDE), the UCI-CDC staff developed an intensive multicomponent program which has four components: (a) intensive (6 hours per day) behavioral intervention conducted by a teacher and a behavioral specialist in a classroom of 12 to 15 students with ADD; (b) daily skill training groups conducted by mixed clinical and educational staff (one counselor and the teacher or aide); (c) careful double-blind assessments of pharmacological interventions which evaluate effects on learning as well as behavior; (d) parent involvement in group and individual meetings to extend the behavior modification to the home-setting.

Based on the literature describing behavioral treatment in special classrooms for disruptive children, the UCI-OCDE program emphasizes non-pharmacological school-based intervention for children with ADD. Progress in this one-year program is associated with movement through three levels of treatment. Level I intervention is based on continuous monitoring of and direct feedback to children using social reinforcers and tokens. An intensity sufficient to have an acute effect on the behavior of even difficult

cases is maintained (typically 2-4 weeks) until success is achieved (defined as earning 90% of possible tokens). Level II intervention is based on self-monitoring and self-evaluation (the "match game"), which is used to fade the continuous monitoring and is intended to foster generalization. The length of time to meet the criteria for matching with a counselor has been variable, requiring from 4 to 16 weeks. Level III intervention is based on self-evaluation using the "match game" and on responsibility/privilege contingencies which reflect the uncertainties of natural consequences in the real world environment. This has been used for long-term (24 to 48 weeks) maintenance of socially appropriate behavior without continuous use of tokens.

Generalization and transfer of behavioral programs have been difficult to demonstrate. To address this critical issue, specific generalization training is provided in three ways. Transfer across settings (from group therapy to classroom) is fostered by mixing staff; the educational staff (teachers and aides) participate in cognitive and social skills training sessions, so they may act as discriminative stimuli and provide appropriate prompts in the classroom. Context-appropriate training is provided; cognitive techniques (e.g., self-evaluation) are integrated into daily classroom and playground activities. Multiple token systems are linked; point values are equated and a common daily summary is used to make reinforcement contingent upon cross-situational behavior. Six to eight group sessions are scheduled to teach parents the basic principles and techniques of behavior modification, and individual meetings are scheduled with a psychologist who supervises the classroom and group interventions with their child with ADD. The purpose of these individual sessions is to build mastery of behavioral techniques and to prepare parents to direct and maintain a permanent treatment program for chronic residual symptoms that are expected to remain in ADD/ODD children even after successful acute treatment in the UCI-OCDE program.

Thus, the coordination of clinical and educational services in the integrated UCI-OCDE program is designed to move severely affected children with ADD through a "levels system" which starts with constant monitoring (level I), graduates to self-monitoring and self-evaluation (level II), and has as its long-term goal withdrawal of the token system and replacement with a responsibility privilege system (level III). After successful completion of the program, usually over a 6 to 9 month period of time, the student with ADD may enter a transition program based in a neighborhood school where the paraprofessional model is used to reacquaint the student with ADD with placement in a regular classroom.

Summary

At the UCI-CDC, the choice of a school-based intervention for a child with ADD is based on the selection from a continuum of interventions for ADD-related problems on the severity of a given child's ADD symptoms and the degree to which this condition impairs educational performance. (PGARD, 1991)

Prevention/Treatment Program For Kindergaren Students With ADD

Model program of the University of Massachusetts Medical Center, Worcester (reprinted from CHADDER, Spring/Summer 1992) by
Terri L. Shelton, Ph.D. Co-Investigator, Assistant Professor of Psychiatry and Pediatrics, University of Massachusetts Medical Center, Worcester, Massachusetts and Cheryl Crosswaite, M.Ed., Educational Consultant, Kindergarten Grant, University of Massachusetts Medical Center, Worcester, Massachusetts

In 1991, Dr. Russell Barkley was awarded a $1.6 million grant from the National Institute of Mental Health in collaboration with the Worcester, Massachusetts Public Schools to design and evaluate a prevention/treatment program for Kindergarten children who had been identified by their parents as being at risk for ADD and oppositional behaviors. With co-investigator Dr. Terri Shelton and educational consultant, Cheryl Crosswaite, M. Ed., this program recently ended the first four months of programming for two classes of Kindergarten children. While follow-up data are not yet available, preliminary analyses and observations indicated that the classroom portion of the intervention program is quite successful.

The program is based on three factors: (1) the empirical research on the needs of children with ADD and effective strategies, (2) pre-existing data from a similar program at the University of California, Irvine under the direction of Dr. James M. Swanson, (3) the developmental strengths and needs of Kindergarten children in general. Because Kindergarten is often a child's first experience to be as successful as possible and for the child to be prepared for first grade-behaviorally, socially, and academically-various aspects of the treatment program are designed to address these three areas.

Behavioral Interventions

Children with attention problems need more frequent, immediate, consistent, and tangible feedback. The periodic report card at the end of the marking period or the comments of the teacher are generally not sufficient for the child with ADD. In this program, the attention and positive behaviors of the children are encouraged and maintained through a very rich system of feedback. There are mechanisms for punishing or reducing undesired behaviors but also strategies for rewarding and encouraging desired behaviors. The program also is flexible enough not to interfere too much with teaching.

We have incorporated a response cost procedure (loss of points) that works well. A key component is a high rate of positive verbal feedback throughout the day. The teacher or aide gives every child at least 10 "big deal" stickers and accompanying verbal feedback per day for positive behaviors (e.g., good attitude, paying attention, working cooperatively, etc.). Periodic classroom observations are conducted to ensure that the positive statements are at least equal to if not exceeding the negatives on a 2:1 basis. This may mean commenting on a child's clothes or their good attitude even if they are not making large gains academically or behaviorally. As mentioned, the "big deals" are awarded for specific target behaviors and are translated into a preferred activity. This activity is contingent on the class achieving a certain number of points. By ensuring that all children receive a minimum number of stickers, it is less competitive and seems to foster a feeling of community. Often students may assist another child in ignoring behaviors if they know that it will result in everyones's getting a desired activity.

The ongoing feedback in the classroom is enhanced in several ways. A tape with a tone that goes off on the average of every 10 minutes is used. When the tone goes off, it is the teacher's and aide's cue to comment on the behavior of everyone. "I see Michael sitting nicely." "I see that Jennifer is looking at me." This type of feedback doesn't take much time and can be integrated easily into teaching.

Another type of feedback is sitting near a child who is having some difficulty to try and "catch the child being good." As children with ADD often have difficulty following rules, the mere physical proximity to the "rules," that is the teacher or aide, seems to help. A reminder by whispering to a child in circle time that she's doing a nice job of listening and a pat or a rub of the back can do a lot to prevent negative behavior from occuring. This strategy is particularly helpful with children who have received a good deal of negative feedback previously or who may have difficulty settling down once a negative behavior has started. The rub of the back as you walk through the class assisting the children with their papers has been amazingly helpful. The physical contact and containment seems to help focus the children.

While there are frequent positive comments, most children with ADD who also have oppositional behaviors require feedback regarding negative behaviors. In this program, negatives are dispensed in a response cost way. Most disruptive classroom behaviors can be categorized into three basic classes of behavior: noncompliance, interrupting, and aggression. Noncompliance is any instance of not following the teacher's direction (e.g., not listening, not finishing an assigned task). Interrupting is self-explanatory, and aggression includes destruction of property, verbal abuse of others, actual hitting, and any touching of others even if it is the pestering touching that often goes on. This type of touching often escalates to fighting so it has been beneficial to address the behavior immediately.

To help the children and staff keep track of the behaviors on an ongoing basis, each child's behavior is addressed immediately and a tally of the behaviors reviewed every 30 minutes using a three-color system. Feedback periods also could be determined by specific classroom activities, (e.g., circle time, morning activities). Toward the end of the grant, these periods will be gradually increased and faded. "Red" is the best and means that the child followed the rules and didn't exhibit any of the negative target behaviors for the period. If a child is noncompliant or interrupts, the child earns a "yellow." "Blues" are given for repeated noncompliance and any aggression. In each classroom there is a board with all the children's names running down the left-hand side with the periods across the top and velcro squares that can be changed to the appropriate color at the end of the feedback period. This provides visual feedback for the child as well. Each child begins the period with red, but can be downgraded to yellow or blue depending on his/her behavior.

At the end of the morning and at the end of the day, those reds, yellows, and blues are translated into activites. These feedback periods will be discontinued by the end of the school year. At the reinforcement time, the children have access to three levels of activities: red activities are the most preferred (as indicated by children's preferences); yellow the next, and blue the least. However, *all* children earn some type of activity. Children who earn access to yellow choose from yellow and blue and children who earn red can choose all activities.

The use of time out has been limited as much as possible. Sometimes time out is not effective because it results in the child's avoiding work. Time out is reserved for when a child demonstrates repeated noncompliance or serious aggression. The time out period is based on one to two minutes for each year of the child's age and getting out of time out is contingent on agreeing to do the thing that resulted in the time out in the first place and in being quiet, at least momentarily.

In other instances, a strategy called "tasks" is employed. When the child gets a yellow or a blue they lose their red status. They also have to write tasks where the child is required to copy over a series of numbers. There is a desk with paper and pencil and the tasks written out. For example, if a child interrupts, the teacher or aide immediately says, "That's interrupting. That's yellow. Write X tasks." More tasks are assigned if the child has

earned a "blue." While the possibility existed that this strategy might discourage children from writing, this has not been our experience. The strategy is effective, stops the negative behavior, prevents the child from escalating to more negative behavior, and gets the chld back into the class and the opportunity for earning positive feedback. The papers are thrown away after the teacher or aide checks to see that they are completed correctly. It doesn't seem to lessen the children's interest in writing but does inadvertantly give them practice in writing which many of these children need. If they do not do the tasks well or are noncompliant, more tasks are added on. Parents receive daily feedback about the child's progress.

Social Skills Training

In Kindergarten, all children must learn to adapt their individual needs to the needs of the class. Riding the bus, finding one's way to the classroom, keeping up with your coat and backpack and getting along with others are tasks facing all children. Children with ADD are often at a disadvantage when meeting these typical developmental tasks. To assist the children in this area, a social skills training component is included in the program. The basis for the program is the Skills Streaming series. The drawback to social skills training in the research literature is that the skills do not generalize to other situations unless generalization is built in. To avoid this drawback, social skills are taught and practiced in detail in class (e.g., 30 minutes every day). Role plays seem to work well as do puppets in demonstrating these skills. Kindergarten children are generally too young to be able to use all the steps of a problem solving approach but this is modeled. While it is difficult for a 5 or 6 year old to generate alternatives to inappropriate responses to a difficult social situation, they can be taught to stop and listen to suggestions offered by the teacher or therapist, thus modeling problem solving, and then have the child implement the chosen behavior. The demonstration of a problem solving approach lays the groundwork for the child's assuming a more active role in problem solving when they become older.

These social skills are reinforced further within the classroom by tying them

into an activity or academic lesson. For example, one target behavior is accepting consequences. Children can be rewarded for "accepting consequences" in morning activities if they demonstrate a positive attitude if they are not chosen to hold the flag. The teachers and the aides, as well as project staff, are involved in teaching the social skills lessons on a rotating basis in order to increase the possibility of noticing these behaviors throughout the day in the classroom. In addition to the daily feedback of the child's progress in the behavioral program, the parents are notified of the particular social skills that are being taught so that they could be watchful and reward any of these skills seen at home.

Academic Curriculum

Kindergarten is a time of important changes in the thinking abilities of children. For example, they are more able to take the perspective of others and begin to understand concepts of time and size more completely. Because of these changes and the variability among children in the rate at which they move through these changes, the task of the Kindergarten teacher and parent is particularly challenging. Some children need more practice in basic preschool skills, while others are ready to read and write. Taking a developmental perspective, the classroom curriculum in this program is designed to meet the child at his/her individual level by providing a sufficient level of challenge to avoid boredom while not overwhelming the child.

As with the social skills training, a problem solving approach is modeled in the teaching. Where possible, children are encouraged to stop, read the directions, check and evaluate their work. Reading and math readiness, science, health, arts, etc. are incorporated as well as exposure to computers. While small group and one-to-one instruction are available, care is taken to provide the children with increasing amounts of group instruction to prepare them for the demands of a regular first-grade class.

Conclusion

In all aspects of the program, efforts are taken to provide the child with ongoing success. Because so many children with ADD are at risk for low self-esteem, it is important for the child to have as many chances to see him/herself succeed.

Section Seven

Parents and Schools Working Together

Parents and Schools Working Together

Identifying A Need

ADD-related difficulties affect children with this disorder at home, at school, and with peers. The child with ADD belongs to parents and educators alike. We are equal partners in helping this child successfully overcome the difficulties brought about by this disability. Although this manual focuses mainly on the school-side of ADD, there is an equally compelling home story.

Many parents feel frustrated, ashamed, guilty, angry, and depressed over their perceived inadequacies as parents. "If I were a better mother or father," the parent thinks, "my child wouldn't behave so poorly or have such difficulty doing things that other children do as a matter of course. I wouldn't yell so much. Or say such angry words that I know only cause my child pain." Many parents send their children to school with the expectation that the educators understand their children and will do a better job.

Somewhere along the line, usually as a result of poor school performance, either the parents or the schools discover the child who has difficulty "getting with the program" has ADD. In this current generation of parents and children, frequently the parents are the first to suspect ADD to be at the root of their child's problems. Often, the diagnosis follows only after the child has experienced significant failure and frustration.

While recent years have evidenced greater public awareness about ADD, presently the vast majority of children diagnosed and treated tend to come more from white, upper-middle and middle class families. Yet, ADD knows no socioeconomic, racial, or ethnic bounds. Children from all walks of life have this disability and suffer from its potentially devastating effects. To date, many of the estimated 3% to 5% of children with this disability must still be identified.

The U.S. Education Department's ADD Policy requiring schools to serve children with ADD offers hope of early diagnosis and management to all children who have this disability. Schools have a vital role to play. By exercising the child-find provisions of the Individuals with Disabilities Education Act (IDEA), schools will be instrumental in ensuring that children who need help, get it. Clearly, the use of appropriate assessment techniques will be an important safeguard against the mis-identification of children who may be experiencing difficulties in school that are not ADD-related.

As more and more schools assume a pro-active role in identifying children suspected of having ADD, other issues will arise. In the current state of affairs, parents of children diagnosed with ADD often assume the role of explaining the disorder to educational personnel and recommending necessary educational interventions. Even in instances where schools initiate the ADD identification and assessment, they often find the parents to be more knowledgeable about ADD than anyone in the school. Schools will soon find the tide turned. Rather than parents convincing educators about ADD, to a much greater extent than currently occurs, schools must face head on the issue of convincing parents that their children need services.

Parent Involvement

In *The ADD Hyperactivity Handbook For Schools*, Dr. Parker observes "Parents can have many different initial reactions to the news that their child is having problems at school. Some parents, frustrated and upset, will become defensive and angry. Overwhelmed and unable to handle more problems, their frustrations may spill over to the school and the teacher."

Denial is a common response which often occurs in conjunction with placing blame upon the school. Many parents do not believe the school's reports of behavioral difficulties, since they may not be experiencing similar problems at home. Additionally, some parents who are unaware that they, too, have ADD, often feel resentful about the miserable school experience they had. The idea of history repeating itself proves threatening. Other parents, having faced difficulties for years with little assistance in handling such problems, find repeated negative reports from schools overwhelming. Still others will be happy to finally learn why their child is experiencing difficulty.

Parents need to be approached with sensitivity and compassion, preferably by someone with whom they have a good rapport. Often, a private, one-to-one meeting in advance of a team meeting will ease the parents' minds by affording the opportunity to ask questions and look for reassurance. Even with such measures, team meetings can often seem like tribunals. Although the child's difficulties brought the need for a meeting or consultation, time should also be given to discussing what the child does well.

When Parents and Schools Disagree

Disagreements usually arise over the following issues. The parents may question the school's credibility and disagree over the extent to which problems exist. Conversely, the school may minimize the parents' concerns about their child. Both parties may disagree over what, if anything, needs to be done. Disagreements are often accompanied by a breakdown in communication resulting in adversarial relations. "Unfortunately, both parties may lose sight of the

> *"Unfortunately, both parties may lose sight of the important issue, specifically the needs of the child."*

important issue, specifically the needs of the child," notes Dr. Greene. A clinical psychologist, Dr. Greene has served as an outside consultant to help parents and schools reach a happy medium for the child's well-being. Using a neutral party knowledgeable about the diagnosis and management of ADD often proves to be an effective means of resolving differences before they escalate into disputes.

A Winning Combination

The management of ADD requires a multi-modal method approach utilizing help from a wide network. Parents, educators, and the child's medical and mental health professionals must all work as partners to maximize the positive effects of interventions. Good communication, cooperation, and mutual problem solving efforts between parents and educators are essential.

A very expedient form of communication is the daily or weekly progress report filled out by the child's teachers. Such reports alleviate one of the more frequent complaints voiced by parents, i.e. "No one told me my child was missing assignments and/or failing tests until it was too late to do anything." Parents can monitor assignments, report difficulties, assist the teacher in modifying tasks, and provide home-based rewards for appropriate behavior and academic progress. Schools also play an important role in assisting parents and prescribing physicians in monitoring the effects of medication when it is used.

Parent Support Groups

Support groups are a valuable tool for parents of children with ADD. Schools can refer parents to these groups for assistance and education. Most groups offer information through seminars at monthly meetings, and an opportunity to network with parents experiencing similar problems. Attendance by educators is welcomed and encouraged.

Many schools also offer monthly meetings for parents of students with special needs. Recently, some schools have undertaken parent training programs to assist parents in the home management of ADD problems. In Baltimore County Public Schools, Baltimore, Maryland, the parent training program is conducted by a team of school personnel, including the school psychologist, nurse, and guidance counselor in collaboration with the local ADD parent support group. Here, knowledgeable professionals offer expertise on a wide variety of issues ranging from proven treatments, to developing behavioral contracts, to troubleshooting over methods of supervising homework and other school-related problems.

Outcome

Studies of children with disabilities demonstrate that outcomes are significantly improved when parents actively participate in the child's education. Children with ADD cannot afford a separation of school and home. Disagreements about the "best" way to handle a given child's problems may arise periodically. Such disagreements ought never interfere with the primary mission, i.e., helping children with ADD to be competent and thereby develop a positive sense of self. No "best" way to handle this disability exists, but we do have principles that guide. One essential principle is that parents and schools need to work with each other for the sake of the child.

Section Eight

ADD

A Brief Summary of School District Legal Obligations and Children's Education Rights

ADD: A Brief Summary of School District Legal Obligations and Children's Education Rights[1]

Prepared by David Aronofsky, Esq.

Background

On September 16, 1991, the U.S. Education Department issued a Policy Clarification Memorandum signed by three Department Assistant Secretaries expressly recognizing children with attention deficit disorders (ADD) as eligible for special education and related services under federal law (See Appendix). This Policy makes clear that children with ADD may qualify for special education and related services *solely* on the basis of their ADD when it impairs their education performance or learning under *both* U.S. Public Law 94-142 (Part B of the Individuals With Disabilities Education Act, or "IDEA");[2] and Section 504 of the federal Rehabilitation Act of 1973[3] It resulted from a Department Notice of Inquiry mandated by Congress the previous year to determine how children with ADD were being educated in U.S. public schools.

The Department's Office For Civil Rights (OCR), responsible for Section 504 enforcement and implementation in U.S. education institutions, had ruled in a number of prior individual cases that children with ADD could meet 504 education assistance requirements to serve their specific ADD disability[5] The Department's Office Of Special Education and Rehabilitative Services (OSERS), responsible for 94-142 enforcement, had been somewhat less clear in its intent to apply 94:142 to ADD. Congress sought to clarify the issue by ordering the Notice of Inquiry.

After reviewing over 2,000 written comments submitted during the 120 day Notice period by parents, educators, health professionals and others, the Department learned that many children with ADD were not receiving free appropriate public education as required by 94-142 or 504; while many others appeared to be receiving assistance unrelated to their specific ADD needs[6] The Department then issued its Policy Clarification Memorandum to eliminate "confusion in the field" over when and if children with ADD must receive special education and related services federally mandated for all public school children with disabilities who require such help on the basis of their disabilities. Instead of making ADD a new federal law disability category, the Department concluded that children suffering *solely* from ADD are already eligible for 94-142 assistance under that law's Other Health Impaired category. The Department also concluded that children with ADD might qualify for assistance under other 94-142 categories when these children meet criteria applicable to the latter; and further concluded that children with ADD could qualify for 504 protection without regard to 94-142 eligibility.

U.S. Education Department ADD Policy Legal Significance

Congress has empowered the U.S. Education Department to interpret and enforce 94-142 Part B (through OSERS) and Section 504 (through OCR). The September 1991 Policy reflects a reasonable interpretation of how these federal statutes apply to children with ADD, long recognized by experts as a serious neurologically-based disability. The U.S. Supreme Court recently reiterated the well-established legal principle, long adhered to by the Education Department itself, that a federal agency's reasonable interpretations of the statutes it administers plus its own agency rules have the force of law and thus legally bind those subject to the statutory and rules requirements[7]

Because 94-142 and 504 apply to all public schools by requiring them to provide certain assistance to all children with disabilities who need it, the Department's September 1991 ADD Policy affirms the legal obligation of all public schools to provide such assistance to children whose ADD adversely affects their educational performance. By clarifying these children's 94-142 and 504 rights, the Department Policy may also entitle them to protections available under other federal and state laws briefly described in Sections F and G below.

What The Department's ADD Policy Requires Under 94-142

IDEA Part B, the primary federal law defining disabled children's education rights, requires U.S. public schools to provide a free appropriate public education for all children with disabilities. Such education must include special education and related services specifically designed to meet each child's unique needs through an individualized education program (IEP). The IEP must accurately reflect the nature and severity of each disability present; describe how each disability adversely affects the child's education (including academic, behavioral and extra-curricular aspects); then record what specific aids and services will be provided to meet the child's unique needs caused by each disability, based upon the most current, comprehensive, multi-disciplinary evaluation.

IDEA Part B further requires public schools to meet each disabled child's needs to the maximum extent appropriate in a regular classroom with the child's non-disabled peers (through support services to be provided the child in such classrooms). Where this cannot be done, public schools must consider a range of additional placement options within the full continuum, including but not limited to a mix of regular and special education classroom services; full-time special education classes in a regular public school; a private school; and home bound instruction. The school district must place the child in the least restrictive environment appropriate to the child's identified needs. The concept of a free appropriate public education under IDEA Part B is to ensure at least a minimum floor level of education. States can, however, exceed this minimum federal floor under more expansive state statutes and some do so.[8] IDEA Part B also anticipates reasonable access to extra-curricular activities available to non-disabled children; and freedom from suspension, expulsion or other disciplinary problems resulting from the child's disability and/or a school's refusal to address the disability's behavioral problems.

IDEA Part B imposes affirmative legal obligations on public schools to identify and evaluate promptly, with a multidisciplinary professional team, children having or suspected of having a disability to determine the child's need for 94-142 special education and related services at no charge to the parents. IDEA Part B also provides procedural legal rights and protections for parents who disagree with either an evaluation or a refusal to evaluate, including the right to an impartial hearing and the right to challenge any adverse decision in court. Families who prevail in court proceedings can recover attorney fees, injunctive relief, and possibly monetary damages[9]

IDEA Part B grants the above rights and protections to all children with disabilities who meet the 94-142 eligibility criteria.[10] The Department's September 1991 ADD Policy provides that children with ADD meet the 94-142 "other health impairment" disability definition when their ADD is a *chronic or acute health problem resulting in limited alertness (i.e. attention) which adversely affects educational performance.* The Policy explicitly states that children with ADD may also qualify for 94-142 assistance *if* (but only if) they satisfy eligibility criteria applicable to other disability categories. As with all 94-142 Part B disabilities, having ADD does not automatically qualify a child for 94-142 assistance. The disability must have an adverse effect on educational performance and the child must need special education. A school district's

failure to evaluate such a child to determine whether and how the ADD adversely affects the child's education could violate 94-142 where there is any evidence of education impairment resulting from this disability.

What The Department's ADD Policy Requires Under 504

Section 504 prohibits discrimination against otherwise qualified persons with disabilities in federally assisted programs and activities solely on the basis of such persons' disabilities. All public schools which receive federal funds must comply with Section 504 anti-discrimination rules by addressing the needs of children with disabilities as adequately as the needs of non-disabled children. Section 504, like 94-142, requires schools to provide children with disabilities a free appropriate public education consisting of regular *or* special education *and* related aids *and* services, all designed to meet the individual student's needs; and subject to adequate evaluation, placement and procedural safeguards comparable to those prescribed under 94-142. Section 504 requires public schools to meet the needs of children with disabilities in regular education classes, through the use of supplementary aids and services, to the maximum extent possible before placement into special education alternatives. Section 504 anticipates that the aids and services will be designed to meet the individual educational needs as adequately as the needs of non-disabled persons are met. Section 504 applies for eligibility purposes to any "physical and mental impairment which substantially limits one or more major life activities," such as learning.[11]

Section 504 protections for disabled children can extend somewhat further than those available under 94-142, since 504 does not require a need for special education resulting from the disability as an eligibility prerequisite. School districts may adopt identical evaluation processes and procedural safeguards for both 94-142 and 504 compliance purposes, but they may *not* deny disabled children special education services under 504 merely because a child fails to meet

94-142 services or needs criteria. A school district's failure to meet 504 obligations can result in a cut-off of federal funds.[12] In addition, parents can obtain monetary damages, injunctive relief and attorney fees for 504 violations independently of whether they have a legal right of action in court under 94-142.[13]

The Department's September 1991 ADD Policy 504 section makes clear that children with ADD enjoy the full range of 504 rights available to other children with disabilities. This means that school districts *must* evaluate a child with ADD if the child's parents believe this disability is impairing the child's education, subject to 504 procedural safeguards. School districts must then make an individualized determination of the child's educational needs for regular *or* special education *or* related aids *and* services on the basis of the evaluation; and provide such services as needed in an individualized education plan. The Department ADD Policy specifically cites some suggested regular education classroom adaptations for children with ADD. School districts would probably be well advised to follow these suggestions (where supported by an evaluation) to assure 504 compliance.

94-142 And 504 Relationship To State Laws Applicable To Education For Children With ADD

IDEA and Section 504 are federal laws applicable to all U.S. public schools. These laws provide *minimum* legal rights for all disabled children to a free appropriate public education. In addition to these federal statutes, however, each state has enacted its own laws defining the educational rights of children with disabilities. These state laws, comprised of statutes enacted by legislatures and regulations adopted by state education departments, incorporate at least the minimum federal prerequisites provided for in 94-142 (and to some extent 504, although most states generally tend to concentrate disabled children education lawmaking efforts on 94-142 implementation). Various states have also opted to provide dis abled children and their families with more legal rights than federal law requires[14]

As for children with ADD, each state has education statutes or regulations which incorporate 94-142 requirements, including (by implication) the U.S. Education Department's September 1991 ADD Policy, into its own laws. Several states have either expressly included ADD into their own education statutes or regulations as a disability, or they are presently in the process of doing so[15]

Even without such explicit inclusion, however, a school district's failure to comply with federal 94-142 requirements for children with ADD will quite possibly result in that district's concurrent violation of its own state education laws applicable to educating all children with ADD[16]

School District Obligations And Children's Rights Under Other Federal Laws Applicable To ADD

Although 94-142, 504 and state laws incorporating one or more of these two federal statutes form the primary bases for identifying school district obligations and children's rights regarding education of children with ADD, two other federal laws also affect these obligations and rights. The Federal Civil Rights Act[17] prohibits public school districts from violating federally protected legal rights under color of state or local law. Federal courts have concluded that violations of disabled children's rights protected under 94-142 and 504 can also result in school district Federal Civil Rights Act liability[18] By including a full panoply of remedies (monetary damages, injunctive relief and attorney fees), the Federal Civil Rights Act may offer an additional basis for legal action to protect the educational rights of children with ADD as set forth in the U.S. Education Department's September 1991 ADD Policy.

The new Americans With Disabilities Act[19] provides yet another potential legal means of requiring all education institutions and systems (public and private), other than those operated by religious

organizations, to meet the specific needs of children with ADD. Title II of the Act, applicable to all public schools, prohibits the denial of educational services, programs or activities to all students with disabilities; and also prohibits discrimination against all such students once enrolled. Title II remedies appear identical to those for 504 violations (and thus also appear to permit Federal Civil Rights Act claims). Courts would almost certainly look to the U.S. Education Department ADD Policy 504 section for guidance on how the Act applies to public school children with ADD.

Title III of the Americans With Disabilities Act, however, applies these anti-discrimination bans to private education institutions (other than those operated by religious organizations)[20]

This means that private schools:

(i) cannot deny access to or impose exclusionary eligibility on persons with disabilities on the basis of their disabilities, unless such persons pose health or safety threats to others and such threats cannot be reasonably eliminated by modifying current practices;

(ii) cannot provide persons with disabilities services or facilities separate or different from those available to non-disabled persons except where such difference is needed to ensure the same service effectiveness levels for disabled and non-disabled persons alike;

(iii) must make reasonable modifications in policies, practices or procedures, including the offer of auxiliary aids and services, where such modifications are needed to meet the needs of persons with disabilities unless such modifications, aids and services would either "fundamentally alter" the school activities or impose undue burdens; and

(iv) must provide education courses and examinations in a manner likely to ensure results reflective of a disabled person's actual achievement level rather than the disability (such as by extending the time period for examinations or modifying course format)[21]

Title III authorizes both U.S. Justice Department Civil Rights Division enforcement by obtaining injunctive relief, fines and monetary damages for legally injured individuals; and private suits for injunctive relief and attorney fees (although private suits against private schools for monetary damages do not appear permissible). As with public schools, courts would likely look to the U.S. Education Department ADD Policy for guidance on how private schools should educate children with ADD. Title III thus appears to impose a new set of legal obligations and rights affecting the private school education of these children.

Concluding Comments

The U.S. Education Department's September 1991 ADD Policy will undoubtedly serve as a catalyst for increasing awareness of both school legal obligations and family rights involving children with ADD. Such increased awareness should result in fewer adversarial legal disputes by helping provide greater certainty over whether and how these children are to be educated.

FOOTNOTES:

1. Prepared by David Aronofsky, Esq., an attorney at the Washington, D.C. law firm of Arent Fox Kintner Plotkin & Kahn, which serves as CH.A.D.D. General Counsel, for CH.A.D.D.'s exclusive use. This is designed to summarize various legal issues affecting the education of children with ADD and should not be construed as legal advice or a legal opinion on specific facts. Readers with particular questions are advised to seek assistance of legal counsel.

2. 20 U.S.C. 1400 et seq.; U.S. Education Department rules codified at 34 C.F.R. 300 et seq.

3. 29 U.S.C. 794 et seq.; U.S. Education Department rules codified at 34 C.F.R. 104 et seq.

4. U.S. Public Law 101-476, Sec. 102.

5. See, e.g., 3 EDUCATION OF THE HANDICAPPED LAW REPORTER 353:201 and 205.

6. See, e.g., U.S. Education Department, Summary of Comments on Special Education for Children With Attention Deficit Disorder: a Report (May 1991).

7. OSHRC v. Martin, 111 S. Ct. 1171, 1176 (1991). The Department has expressly stated that it "regards the clarifications and interpretations" of its own statutes and regulations, especially 94-142, "as legally binding...in determining whether affected [state and local education] agencies"are in compliance with the Act and regulations." 46 Federal Register 5460 (Jan. 19, 1981).

8. *See e.g., Conklin v. Anne Arundel County Bd. of Education,* 946 F.2d 306, 308 (4th Cir. 1991) (94-142 "conceived only to provide a federal floor" of minimum educational rights, although states can provide for additional rights and requirements).

9. *See* 20 U.S.C. 1415(e), (f).

10. 20 U.S.C. 1401(a)(1); 34 C.F.R. 300.5(b)(1)-(11).

11. 34 C.F.R. 104.3(j).

12. *Freeman v. Cavazos,* 939 F.2d 1527 (11th Cir. 1991).

13. 29 U.S.C. 794 and 794a; *Franklin v. Gwinnett County Public Schools,* 112 S. Ct. 1028 (1992); *see also I.D. v. Westmoreland School District,* 788 F. Supp. 634, 639-40 (D.N.H. 1992) (recognizing 504 claim even while dismissing one under 94-142).

14. *See, e.g., Conklin, ibid.* and examples cited therein.

15. *See, e.g.,* 1991-92 California Assembly Bill 2773 (adding ADD to Education Code to codify September 1991 U.S. Education Department ADD Policy); Colorado Board of Education Regulation 2220-R-1.01(1) (adding ADD to state 94-142 implementation regulations); Delaware Board of Education Rule I.E.2.c(4) (containing ADD as part of 94-142 and state law learning disabilities definition); 1992 Louisiana Acts 386 and 458 (adding ADD to state education statutes implementing both 94-142 and 504, while also requiring public schools to offer ADD specific education programs); Pennsylvania Board of Education Rule 342.1(a) (including "deficiencies in...attention, impulsivity" within 94-142 specific learning disabilities definition); and October 2, 1991 Virginia Superintendent of Public Instruction Memorandum recognizing the U.S. Department of Education policy and announcing an intent to add ADD to the state 94-142 other health impaired rule. Whether these individual state legal approaches reflect full compliance with federal legal requirements under 94-142 and 504, as manifested in the U.S. Education Department's September 1991 ADD Policy, remains subject to future determination on a state-by-state basis by the courts or the U.S. Department of Education.

16. *See Conklin, ibid.,* for analysis of when 94-142 violations might concurrently violate state education laws.

17. 42 U.S.C. 1983, 1988.

18. *Digre v. Roseville Schools Ind. Dist. No. 623,* 841 F.2d, 249 (8th Cir. 1988) (permitting § 1983 action for 94-142 violation); *Pendleton v. Jefferson Local School Dist.,* 754 F. Supp. 570, 576 (S.D. Ohio 1990), and *Sanders v. Marquette Public Schools,* 561 F. Supp 1361 (W.D. *Mich.* 1983) (permitting § 1983 suits for 504 violations).

19. 42 U.S.C. 12101 et seq.

20. 42 U.S.C. 12181(7)(j), 12182.

21. 42 U.S.C. 12189.

Appendix

1. **US Department of Education Policy Memorandum on Attention Deficit Disorders**

2. **CH.A.D.D. Guide to Medical Management**

3. **Controversial Treatments for Children With Attention Deficit Hyperactivity Disorder**

UNITED STATES DEPARTMENT OF EDUCATION

OFFICE OF SPECIAL EDUCATION AND REHABILITATIVE SERVICES

THE ASSISTANT SECRETARY

MEMORANDUM

SEP I 6 1991

DATE   :

TO   :   Chief State School Officers

FROM   :   Robert R. Davila
                Assistant Secretary
                Office of Special Education
                    and Rehabilitative Services

                Michael L. Williams
                Assistant Secretary
                Office for Civil Rights

                John T. MacDonald
                Assistant Secretary
                Office of Elementary
                    and Secondary Education

SUBJECT   :   Clarification of Policy to Address the Needs of
                Children with Attention Deficit Disorders within
                General and/or Special Education

I.   Introduction

There is a growing awareness in the education community that attention deficit disorder (ADD) and attention deficit hyperactive disorder (ADHD) can result in significant learning problems for children with those conditions. While estimates of the prevalence of ADD vary widely, we believe that three to five percent of school-aged children may have significant educational problems related to this disorder. Because ADD has broad implications for education as a whole, the Department believes it should clarify State and local responsibility under Federal law for addressing the needs of children with ADD in the schools. Ensuring that these students are able to reach their fullest potential is an inherent part of the National education goals and AMERICA 2000. The National goals, and the strategy for achieving them, are based on the assumptions that: (1) all children can learn and benefit from their education; and (2) the educational community must work to improve the learning opportunities for all children.

---

[1] While we recognize that the disorders ADD and ADHD vary, the term ADD is being used to encompass children with both disorders.

MARYLAND AVE. S.W. WASHINGTON D.C.

This memorandum clarifies the circumstances under which children with ADD are eligible for special education services under Part B of the Individuals with Disabilities Education Act (Part B), as well as the Part B requirements for evaluation of such children's unique educational needs. This memorandum will also clarify the responsibility of State and local educational agencies (SEAs and LEAs) to provide special education and related services to eligible children with ADD under Part B. Finally, this memorandum clarifies the responsibilities of LEAs to provide regular or special education and related aids and services to those children with ADD who are not eligible under Part B, but who fall within the definition of "handicapped person" under Section 504 of the Rehabilitation Act of 1973. Because of the overall educational responsibility to provide services for these children, it is important that general and special education coordinatetheir efforts.

II.   Eligibility for Special Education and Related Services under Part B

Last year during the reauthorization of the Education of the Handicapped Act (now the Individuals with Disabilities Education Act), Congress gave serious consideration to including ADD in the definition of "children with disabilities" in the statute. The Department took the position that ADD does not need to be added as a separate disability category in the statutory definition since children with ADD who require special education and related services can meet the eligibility criteria for services under Part B. This continues to be the Department's position.

No change with respect to ADD was made by Congress in the statutory definition of "children with disabilities;" however, language was included in Section 102(a) of the Education of the Handicapped Act Amendments of 1990 that required the Secretary to issue a Notice of Inquiry (NOI) soliciting public comment on special education for children with ADD under Part B. In response to the NOI (published November 29, 1990 in the Federal Register), the Department received over 2000 written comments, which have been transmitted to the Congress. Our review of these written comments indicates that there is confusion in the field regarding the extent to which children with ADD may be served in special education programs conducted under Part B.

A.   Description of Part B

Part B requires SEAs and LEAs to make a free appropriate public education (FAPE) available to all eligible children with disabilities and to ensure that the rights and protections of Part B are extended to those children and their parents 20 U.S.C. 1412(2); 34 CFR SS300.121 and 300.2. Under Part B, FAPE, among other elements, includes the provision of special education and related services, at no cost to parents, in conformity with an individualized education program (IEP). 34 CFR §300.4.

In order to be eligible under Part B, a child must be evaluated in accordance with 34 CFR §§300.530-300.534 as having one or more specified physical or mental impairments, and must be found to require special education and related services by reason of one or more of these impairments.[2] 20 U.S.C. 1401 (a) (1); 34 CFR §300.5. SEAs and LEAs must ensure that children with ADD who are determined eligible for services under Part B receive special education and related services designed to meet their unique needs, including special education and related services needs arising from the ADD. A full continuum of placement alternatives, including the regular classroom, must be available for providing special education and related services required in the IEP.

B.   Eligibility for Part B services under the "Other Health Impaired" Category

The list of chronic or acute health problems included within the definition of "other health impaired" in the Part B regulations is not exhaustive. The term "other health impaired" includes chronic or acute impairments that result in limited alertness, which adversely affects educational performanc. Thus, children with ADD should be classified as eligible for services under the "other health impaired" category in instances where the ADD is a chronic or acute health problem that results in limited alertness. which adversely affects educational performance. In other words, children with ADD, where the ADD is a chronic or acute health problem resulting in limited alertness, may be considered disabled under Part B solely on the basis of this disorder within the "other health impaired" category in situations where special education and related services are needed because of the ADD.

---

[2] The Part B regulations define 11 specified disabilities. 34 CFR §300.5(b) (1)-(11). The Education of the Handicapped Act Amendments of 1990 amended the Individuals with Disabilities Education Act (formerly the Education of the Handicapped Act) to specify that autism and traumatic brain injury are separate disability categories. See section 602(a) (1) of the Act, to be codified at 20 U.S.C. 1401(a) (1).

C.   Eligibility for Part B services under Other Disability Categories

Children with ADD are also eligible for services under Part B if the children satisfy the criteria applicable to other disability categories. For example, children with ADD are also eligible for services under the "specific learning disability" category of Part B if they meet the criteria stated in §§300.5(b) (9) and 300.541 or under the "seriously emotionally disturbed" category of Part B if they meet the criteria stated i §300.5(b) (8).

III.   Evaluations under Part B

A.   Requirements

SEAs and LEAs have an affirmative obligation to evaluate a child who is suspected of having a disability to determine the child's need for special education and related services. Under Part B, SEA's and LEAs are required to have procedures for locating, identifying and evaluating all children who have a disability or are suspected of having a disability and are in need of special education and related services. 34 CFR §§300.128 and 300.220. This responsibility, known as "child find," is applicable to all children from birth through 21, regardless of the severity of their disability.

Consistent with this responsibility and the obligation to make FAPE available to all eligible children with disabilities, SEAs and LEAs must ensure that evaluations of children who are suspected of needing special education and related services are conducted without undue delay. 20 U.S.C. 1412(2). Because of its responsibility resulting from the FAPE and child find requirements of Part B, an LEA may not refuse to evaluate the possible need for special education and related services of a child with a prior medical diagnosis of ADD solely by reason of that medical diagnosis. However, a medical diagnosis of ADD alone is not sufficient to render a child eligible for services under Part B.

Under Part B, before any action is taken with respect to the initial placement of a child with a disability in a program providing special education and related services, "a full and individual evaluation of the child's educational needs must be conducted in accordance with requirements of §300.532." 34 CFR §300.531. Section 300.532(a) requires that a child's evaluation must be conducted by a multidisciplinary team, including at least one teacher or other specialist with knowledge in the area of suspected disability.

B.   Disagreements over Evaluations

Any proposal or refusal of an agency to initiate or change the identification, evaluation, or educational placement of the child, or the provision of FAPE to the child is subject to the written prior notice requirements of 34 CFR §§300.504-300.505.[3] If a parent disagrees with the LEA's refusal to evaluate a child or the LEA's evaluation and determination that a child does not have a disability for which the child is eligible for services under Part B, the parent may request a due process hearing pursuant to 34 CFR §§300.506-300.513 of the Part B regulations.

IV.   Obligations Under Section 504 of SEAs and LEAs to Children with ADD Found Not To Require Special Education and Related Services under Part B

Even if a child with ADD is found not to be eligible for services under Part B, the requirements of Section 504 of the Rehabilitation Act of 1973 (Section 504) and its implementing regulation at 34 CFR Part 104 may be applicable. Section 504 prohibits

---

[3] Section 300.505 of the Part B regulations sets out the elements that must be contained in the prior written notice to parents:

(1) A full explanation of all of the procedural safeguards available to the parents under Subpart E;
(2) A description of the action proposed or refused by the agency, an explanation of why the agency proposes or refuses to take the action, and a description of any options the agency considered and the reasons why those options were rejected;
(3) A description of each evaluation procedure, test, record, or report the agency uses as a basis for the proposal or refusal; and
(4) A description of any other factors which are relevant to the agency's proposal or refusal.

34 CFR §300.505(a) (1)-(4).

discrimination on the basis of handicap by recipients of Federal funds. Since Section 504 is a civil rights law, rather than a funding law, its requirements are framed in different terms than those of Part B. While the Section 504 regulation was written with an eye to consistency with Part B, it is more general, and there are some differences arising from the differing natures of the two laws. For instance, the protections of Section 504 extend to some children who do not fall within the disability categories specified in Part B.

A.   Definition

Section 504 requires every recipient that operates a public elementary or secondary education program to address the needs of children who are considered "handicapped persons" under Section 504 as adequately as the needs of nonhandicapped persons are met. "Handicapped person" is defined in the Section 504 regulation as any person who has a physical or mental impairment which substantially limits a major life activity (e.g., learning). 34 CFR §104.3(j). Thus, depending on the severity of their condition, children with ADD may fit within that definition.

B.   Programs and Services Under Section 504

Under Section 504, an LEA must provide a free appropriate public education to each qualified handicapped child. A free appropriate public education, under Section 504, consists of regular or special education and related aids and services that are designed to meet the individual student's needs and based on adherence to the regulator requirements on educational setting, evaluation, placement, and procedural safeguards. 34 CFR §§104.33, 104.34, 104.35, and 104.36. A student may be handicapped within the meaning of Section 504, and therefore entitled to regular or special education and related aids and services under the Section 504 regulation, even though the student may not be eligible for special education and related services under Part B.

Under Section 504, if parents believe that their child is handicapped by ADD, the LEA must evaluate the child to determine whether he or she is handicapped as defined by Section 504. If an LEA determines that a child is not handicapped under Section 504, the parent has the right to contest that determination. If the child is determined to be handicapped under Section 504, the LEA must make an individualized determination of the child's educational needs for regular or special education or related aids and services. 34 CFR §104.35. For children determined to be handicapped under Section 504, implementation of an individualized education program developed in accordance with

Part B, although not required, is one means of meeting the free appropriate public education requirements of Section 504.[4] The child's education must be provided in the regular education classroom unless it is demonstrated that education in the regular environment with the use of supplementary aids and services cannot be achieved satisfactorily. 34 CFR §104.34.

Should it be determined that the child with ADD is handicapped for purposes of Section 504 and needs only adjustments in the regular classroom, rather than special education, those adjustments are required by Section 504. A range of strategies is available to meet the educational needs of children with ADD. Regular classroom teachers are important in identifying the appropriate educational adaptions and interventions for many children with ADD.

SEAs and LEAs should take the necessary steps to promote coordination between special and regular education programs. Steps also should be taken to train regular education teachers and other personnel to develop their awareness about ADD and its manifestations and the adaptations that can be implemented in regular education programs to address the instructional needs of these children. Examples of adaptations in regular education programs could include the following:

> providing a structured learning environment; repeating and simplifying instructions about in-class and homework assignments; supplementing verbal instructions with visual instructions; using behavioral management techniques; adjusting class schedules; modifying test delivery; using tape recorders, computer-aided instrction, and other audiovisual equipment; selecting modified textbooks or workbooks; and tailoring homework assignments.

Other provisions range from consultation to special resources and may include reducing class size; use of one-on-one tutorials; classroom aides and note takers; involvement of a "services coordinator" to oversee implementation of special programs and services, and possible modification of nonacademic times such as lunchroom, recess, and physical education.

Through the use of appropriate adaptations and interventions in regular classes, many of which may be required by Section 504, the Department believes that LEAs will be able to effectively address the instructional needs of many children with ADD.

---

[4]Many LEAs use the same process for determining the needs of students under Section 504 that they use for implementing Part B.

C.   Procedural Safeguards Under Section 504

Procedural safeguards under the Section 504 regulation are stated more generally than in Part B. The Section 504 regulation requires the LEA to make available a system of procedural safeguards that permits parents to challenge actions regarding the identification, evaluation, or educational placement of their handicapped child whom they believe needs special education or related services. 34 CFR §104.36. The Section 504 regulation requires that the system of procedural safeguards include notice, an opportunity for the parents or guardian to examine relevant records, an impartial hearing with opportunity for participation by the parents or guardian and representation by counsel, and a review procedure. Compliance with procedural safeguards of Part B is one means of fulfilling the Section 504 requirements.[5] However, in an impartial due process hearing raising issues under the Section 504 regulation, the impartial hearing officer must make a determination based upon that regulation.

V.   Conclusion

Congress and the Department have recognized the need to provide information and assistance to teachers, administrators, parents and other interested persons regarding the identification, evaluation, and instructional needs of children with ADD. The Department has formed a work group to explore strategies across principal offices to address this issue. The work group also plans to identify some ways that the Department can work with the education associations to cooperatively consider the programs and services needed by children with ADD across special and regular education.

In fiscal year 1991, the Congress appropriated funds for the Department to synthesize and disseminate current knowledge related to ADD. Four centers will be established in Fall, 1991 to analyze and synthesize the current research literature on ADD relating to identification, assessment, and interventions. Research syntheses will be prepared in formats suitable for educators, parents and researchers. Existing clearinghouses and networks, as well as Federal, State and local organizations will be utilized to disseminate these research syntheses to parents, educators and administrators, and other interested persons.

---

[5] Again, many LEAs and some SEAs are conserving time and resources by using the same due process procedures for resolving disputes under both laws.

In addition, the Federal Resource Center will work with SEAs and the six regional resource centers authorized under the Individuals with Disabilities Education Act to identfy effective identification and assesment procedures, as well as intervention strategies being implemented across the country for children with ADD. A document describing current practice will be developed and disseminated to parents, educators and administrators, and other interested persons through the regional resource centers, network, as well as by parent training centers, other parent and consumer organizations, and professional organizations. Also, the Office for Civil Rights' ten regional offices stand ready to provide technical assistance to parents and educators.

It is our hope that the above information will be of assistance to your State as you plan for the needs of children with ADD who require special education and related services under Part B, as well as for the needs of the broader group of children with ADD who do not qualify for special education and related services under Part B, but for whom special education or adaptations in regular education programs are needed. If you have any questions, please contact Jean Peelen, Office for Civil Rights; (Phone: 202/732-1635), Judy Schrag, Office of Special Education Programs (Phone: 202/732-1007); or Dan Bonner, Office of Elementary and Secondary Education (Phone: 202/401-0984).

Medical Management of Children with Attention Deficit Disorders
Commonly Asked Questions

by

Children with Attention Deficit Disorders (CH.A.D.D.)
American Academy of Child and Adolescent Psychiatry (AACAP)

Harvey C. Parker, Ph.D.
CH.A.D.D., Executive Director

George Storm, M.D.
CH.A.D.D., Professional Advisory Board

Committee of Community Psychiatry and Consultation to Agencies of AACAP
Theodore A. Petti, M.D., M.P.H., Chairperson
Virginia Q. Anthony, AACAP, Executive Director

1. What is an Attention Deficit Disorder.

Attention deficit disorder (ADD), also known as attention deficit hyperactivity disorder (ADHD), is a treatable disorder which affects approximately three to five per cent of the population. Inattentiveness, impulsivity, and oftentimes, hyperactivity, are common characteristics of the disorder. Boys with ADD tend to outnumber girls by three to one, although ADD in girls is underidentified.

Some common symptoms of ADD are:

1. Excessively fidgets or squirms
2. Difficulty remaining seated
3. Easily distracted
4. Difficulty awaiting turn in games
5. Blurts out answers to questions
6. Difficulty following instructions
7. Difficulty sustaining attention

8. Shifts from one activity to another
9. Difficulty playing quietly
10. Often talks excessively
11. Often interrupts
12. Often doesn't listen to what is said
13. Often loses things
14. Often engages in dangerous activities

However, you don't have to be hyperactive to have an attention deficit disorder. In fact, up to 30% of children with ADD are not hyperactive at all, but still have a lot of trouble focusing attention.

2. How can we tell if a child has ADD?

Many factors can cause children to have problems paying attention besides an attention deficit disorder. Family problems, stress, discouragement, drugs, physical illness, and learning difficulties can all cause problems that look like ADD, but really aren't. To accurately identify whether a child has ADD, a comprehensive evaluation needs to be performed by professionals who are familiar with characteristics of the disorder.

STRESS
DISCOURAGEMENT
PHYSICAL ILLNESS
LEARNING DIFFICULTIES
FAMILY PROBLEMS

The process of evaluating whether a child has ADD usually involves a variety of professionals which can include the family physician, pediatrician, child and adolescent psychiatrist or psychologist, neurologist, family counselor and teacher. Psychiatric interview, psychological and educational testing, and/or a neurological examination can provide information leading to a proper diagnosis and treatment planning. An accurate evaluation is necessary before proper treatment can begin. Complex cases in which the diagnosis is unclear or is complicated by other medical and psychiatric conditions should be seen by a physician.

Parents and teachers, being the primary sources of information about the child's ability to attend and focus at home and in school, play an integral part in the evaluation process.

3. What kinds of services and programs help children with ADD and their families?

Help for the ADD child and the family is best provided through *multi-modal* treatment delivered by a team of professionals who look after the medical, emotional, behavioral, and educational needs of the child. Parents play an essential role as coordinators of services and programs designed to help their child. Such services and programs may include:

- Medication to help improve attention, and reduce impulsivity and hyperactivity, as well as to treat other emotional or adjustment problems which sometimes accompany ADD.

- Training parents to understand ADD and to be more effective behavior managers as well as advocates for their child.

- Counseling or training ADD children in methods of self-control, attention focusing, learning strategies, organizational skills, or social skill development.

- Psychotherapy to help the demoralized or even depressed ADD child.

- Other interventions at home and at school designed to enhance self-esteem and foster acceptance, approval, and a sense of belonging.

4. What medications are prescribed for ADD children?

Medications can dramatically improve attention span and reduce hyperactive and impulsive behavior. Psychostimulants have been used to treat attentional deficits in children since the 1940's. Antidepressants, while used less frequently to treat ADD, have been shown to be quite effective for the management of this disorder in some children.

5. How do psychostimulants such as Dexedrine (dextroamphetamine), Ritalin (methylphenidate) and Cylert (pemoline) help?

Seventy to eighty per cent of ADD children respond in a positive manner to psychostimulant medication. Exactly how these medicines work is not known. However, benefits for children can be quite significant and are most apparent when concentration is required. In classroom settings, on-task behavior and completion of assigned tasks is increased, socialization with peers and teacher is improved, and disruptive behaviors (talking out, demanding attention, getting out of seat, noncompliance with requests, breaking rules) are reduced.

The specific dose of medicine must be determined for each child. Generally, the higher the dose, the greater the effect and side effects. To ensure proper dosage, regular monitoring at different levels should be done. Since there are no clear guidelines as to how long a child should take medication, periodic trials off medication should be done to determine continued need. Behavioral rating scales, testing on continuous performance tasks, and the child's self-reports provide helpful, but not infallible measures of progress.

Despite myths to the contrary, a positive response to stimulants is often found in adolescents with ADD, therefore, medication need not be discontinued as the child reaches adolescence if it is still needed.

6. What are common side effects of psychostimulant medications?

Reduction in appetite, loss of weight, and problems in falling asleep are the most common adverse effects. Children treated

with stimulants may become irritable and more sensitive to criticism or rejection. Sadness and a tendency to cry are occasionally seen.

The unmasking or worsening of a tic disorder is an infrequent effect of stimulants. In some cases this involves Tourette's Disorder. Generally, except in Tourette's, the tics decrease or disappear with the discontinuation of the stimulant. Caution must be employed in medicating adolescents with stimulants if there are coexisting disorders, e.g. depression, substance abuse, conduct, tic or mood disorders. Likewise, caution should be employed when a family history of a tic disorder exists.

Some side effects, e.g. decreased spontaneity, are felt to be dose-related and can be alleviated by reduction of dosage or switching to another stimulant. Similarly, slowing of height and weight gain of children on stimulants has been documented, with a return to normal for both occurring upon discontinuation of the medication. Other less common side effects have been described but they may occur as frequently with a placebo as with active medication. Pemoline may cause impaired liver functioning in 3% of children, and this may not be completely reversed when this medication is discontinued.

Over-medication has been reported to cause impairment in cognitive functioning and alertness. Some children on higher doses of stimulants will experience what has been described as a "rebound" effect, consisting of changes in mood, irritability and increases of the symptoms associated with their disorder. This occurs with variable degrees of severity during the late afternoon or evening, when the level of medicine in the blood falls. Thus, an additional low dose of medicine in the late afternoon or a decrease of the noontime dose might be required.

7. When are tricyclic antidepressants such as Tofranil (imipramine), Norpramin (desipramine) and Elavil (amytriptyline) used to treat ADD children?

This group of medications is generally considered when contraindications to stimulants exist, when stimulants have not been effective or have resulted in unacceptable side effects, or when the antidepressant property is more critical to treatment than the decrease of inattentiveness. They are used much less freguenlty than the stimulants, seem to have a different mechanism of action, and may be somewhat less effective than the psychostimulants in treating ADD. Long-term use of the tricyclics has not been well studied. Children with ADD who are also experiencing anxiety or depression may do best with an initial trial of a tricyclic antidepressant followed, if needed, with a stimulant for the more classic ADD symptoms.

8. What are the side effects of tricyclic antidepressant medications?

Side effects include constipation and dry mouth. Symptomatic treatment with stool softeners and sugar free gum or candy are usually effective in alleviating the discomfort. Confusion, elevated blood pressure, possible precipitation of manic-like behavior and inducement of seizures are uncommon side effects. The latter three occur in vulnerable individuals who can generally be identified during the assessment phase.

9. What about ADD children who do not respond well to medication?

Some ADD children or adolescents will not respond satisfactorily to either the psychostimulant or tricyclic antidepressant medications. Non-responders may have severe symptoms of ADD, may have other problems in addition to ADD, or may not be able to tolerate certain medications due to adverse side effects as noted above. In such cases consultation with a child and adolescent psychiatrist may be helpful.

10. How often should medications be dispensed at school to an ADD child?

Since the duration for effective action for Ritalin and Dexedrine, the most commonly used psychostimulants, is only about four hours, a second dose during school is often required. Taking a second dose of medication at noon-time enables the ADD child to focus attention effectively, utilize appropriate school behavior and maintain academic productivity. However, the noon-time dose can sometimes be eliminated for children whose afternoon academic schedule does not require high levels of attentiveness. Some psychostimulants, i.e. SR Ritalin (sustained release form) and Cylert, work for longer periods of time (eight to ten hours) and may help avoid the need for a noon-time dose. Antidepressant medications used to treat ADD are usually taken in the morning, afternoon hours after school, or in the evening.

In many cases the physician may recommend that medication be continued at non-school times such as weekday afternoons, weekends or school vacations. During such non-school times lower doses of medication than those taken for school may be sufficient. It is important to remember that ADD is more than a school problem — it is a problem which often interferes in the learning of constructive social, peer, and sports activities.

11. How should medication be dispensed at school?

Most important, regardless of who dispenses medication, since an ADD child may already feel "different" from others, care should be taken to provide discreet reminders to the child when it is time to take medication. It is quite important that school personnel treat the administration of medication in a sensitive manner, thereby safeguarding the privacy of the child or adolescent and avoiding any unnecessary embarrassment. Success in doing this will increase the student's compliance in taking medication.

The location for dispensing medication at school may vary depending upon the school's resources. In those schools with a full-time nurse, the infirmary would be the first choice. In those schools in which a nurse is not always available, other properly trained school personnel may take the responsibility of supervising and dispensing medication.

12. How should the effectiveness of medication and other treatments for the ADD child be monitored?

Important information needed to judge the effectiveness of medication usually comes from reports by the child's parents and teachers and should include information about the child's behavior and attentiveness, academic performance, social and emotional adjustment and any medication side-effects.

Reporting from these sources may be informal through telephone, or more objective via the completion of scales designed for this purpose.

The commonly used teacher rating scales are:
- Conners Teacher Rating Scales
- ADD-H Comprehensive Teacher Rating Scale
- Child Behavior Checklist
- ADHD Rating Scale
- Child Attention Problems (CAP) Rating Scale
- School Situations Questionnaire

Academic performance should be monitored by comparing classroom grades prior to and after treatment.

It is important to monitor changes in peer relationships, family functioning, social skills, a capacity to enjoy leisure time, and self-esteem.

The parents, school nurse or other school personnel responsible for dispensing or overseeing the medication trial should have regular contact by phone with the prescribing physician. Physician office visits of sufficient frequency to monitor treatment are critical in the overall care of children with ADD.

13. What is the role of the teacher in the care of children with ADD?

Teaching an ADD child can test the limits of any educator's time and patience. As any parent of an ADD child will tell you, being on the front lines helping these children to manage on a daily basis can be both challenging and exhausting. It helps if teachers know what to expect and if they receive in-service training on how to teach

and manage ADD students in their classroom.

Here are some ideas that teachers told us have helped:
- Build upon the child's strengths by offering a great deal of encouragement and praise for the child's efforts, no matter how small.
- Learn to use behavior modification programs that motivate students to focus attention, behave better, and complete work.
- Talk with the child's parents and find helpful strategies that have worked with the child in the past.
- If the child is taking medication, communicate frequently with the physician (and parents) so that proper adjustments can be made with respect to type or dose of medication. Behavior rating scales are good for this purpose.
- Modify the classroom structure to accommodate the child's span of attention, i.e. shorter assignments, preferential seating in the classroom, appealing curriculum material, animated presentation of lessons, and frequent positive reinforcement.
- Determine whether the child can be helped through special educational resources within the school.
- Consult with other school personnel such as the guidance counselor, school psychologist, or school nurse to get their ideas as well.

14. What are common myths associated with ADD medications?

Myth: Medication should be stopped when a child reaches teen years.
Fact: Research clearly shows that there is continued benefit to medication for those teens who meet criteria for diagnosis of ADD.
Myth: Children build up a tolerance to medication.
Fact: Although the dose of medication may need adjusting from time to time there is no evidence that children build up a tolerance to medication.
Myth: Taking medication for ADD leads to greater likelihood of later drug addiction.
Fact: There is no evidence to indicate that ADD medication leads to an increased likelihood of later drug addiction.

Myth: Positive response to medication is confirmation of a diagnosis of ADD.
Fact: The fact that a child shows improvement of attention span or a reduction of activity while taking ADD medication does not substantiate the diagnosis of ADD. Even some normal children will show a marked improvement in attentiveness when they take ADD medications.
Myth: Medication stunts growth.
Fact: ADD medications may cause an initial and mild slowing of growth, but over time the growth suppression effect is minimal if non-existent in most cases.
Myth: Taking ADD medications as a child makes you more reliant on drugs as an adult.
Fact: There is no evidence of increased medication taking when medicated ADD children become adults, nor is there evidence that ADD children become addicted to their medications.
Myth: ADD children who take medication attribute their success only to medication.
Fact: When self-esteem is encouraged, a child taking medication attributes his success not only to the medication but to himself as well.

Summary of Important Points

1. ADD children make up 3-5% of the population, but many children who have trouble paying attention may have problems other than ADD. A thorough evaluation can help determine whether attentional deficits are due to ADD or to other conditions.

2. Once identified, ADD children are best treated with a *multi-modal* approach. Best results are obtained when behavioral management programs, educational interventions, parent training, counseling, and medication, when needed, are used together to help the ADD child. Parents of children and adolescents with ADD play the key role of coordinating these services.

3. Each ADD child responds in his or her own unique way to medication depending upon the child's physical make-up, severity of ADD symptoms, and other possible problems accompanying the ADD. Responses to medication need to be monitored and reported to the child's physician.

4. Teachers play an essential role in helping the ADD child feel comfortable within the classroom procedures and work demands, sensitivity to self-esteem issues, and frequent parent-teacher contact can help a great deal.

5. ADD may be a life-long disorder requiring life-long assistance. Families, and the children themselves, need our continued support and understanding.

6. Successful treatment of the medical aspects of ADD is dependent upon ongoing collaboration between the prescribing physician, teacher, therapist and parents.

Controversial Treatments for Children with Attention Deficit Hyperactivity Disorder

Sam Goldstein, Ph.D.
Neurology, Learning and Behavior Center
University of Utah School of Medicine
Salt Lake City, Utah
and
Barbara Ingersoll, Ph.D.
Montgomery Child and Family Health Services, Inc., Bethesda, Maryland
West Virginia University, Departments of Behavioral Medicine and Psychiatry

INTRODUCTION

In the past decade, there has been a tremendous upsurge of scientific and public interest in Attention Deficit Hyperactivity Disorder (ADHD). This interest is reflected not only in the number of scientific articles but in the explosion of books and articles for parents and teachers. Great strides have been made in understanding and managing this disorder. Children with ADHD who would have gone unrecognized and untreated only a few short years ago are now being helped, sometimes with dramatic results.

Psychologist and researcher Dr. Michael Gordon, at State University of New York, Syracuse, has commented that parents should seek the best in evaluation before seeking the best in treatment. Symptoms of inattention, restlessness, impulsivity, and social and academic difficulties can reflect a variety of childhood disorders. It is essential to obtain a thorough understanding of the problem before attempting to intervene, especially since many children with ADHD also experience co-existing learning and behavior problems. A good treatment plan follows logically from a thorough evaluation.

There are still many questions to be answered concerning the development course, outcome and treatment of ADHD. Although there are a number of effective treatments, they are not equally effective with all ADHD children. In their efforts to seek effective help for their children, parents may become desperate. In their desperation, and confused by misinformation, they may turn to treatments which claim to be useful, but which have not been shown to be truly effective, in accord with standards held by the scientific community.

Unfortunately, most parents — no matter how intelligent, well-educated or concerned — do not have the training or expertise necessary to identify and evaluate relevant scientific findings concerning the effectiveness of various treatments which have not, as yet, met scientific standards for effectiveness. Some of these treatments merit continued research; others do not. We do not recommend these as proven treatments. We know that parents need to be informed about them because they may be offered as proven and accepted approaches to the treatment of ADHD, which they are not.

How Are New Treatments Evaluated?

The road by which a particular treatment is shown to be effective can be long and arduous. The process begins with the formulation of a hypothesis, or idea. This hypothesis is usually based upon an existing body of knowledge (e.g. "Since stimulant medication helps ADHD children, it might also help ADHD adults").

The second step is the development of a protocol to evaluate the effectiveness of the proposed treatment. The treatment itself, and the way in which it will be implemented must be carefully defined (e.g. "X amount of medication will be provided to Y number of adults with histories of ADHD for Z period of time").

The researcher must also specify the way in which the effectiveness of the treatment will be evaluated. Care must be taken,

> "In their efforts to seek effective help for their children, parents may become desperate. In their desperation, and confused by misinformation, they may turn to treatments which claim to be useful, but which have not been shown to be truly effective."

for example, to be sure that the effects of the treatment are not due simply to placebo effect. Placebo, which is Latin for "I shall please," refers to the very well documented fact that people may respond to all sorts of ineffective treatments as long as they believe that the treatment has the power to help them. Placebo effects can be more dramatic than most people realize. In a classic example, a drug known to cause vomiting actually brought relief to people suffering from severe nausea and vomiting when they were told it would help them.

The researcher must also take care that all who participate — researchers and research subjects alike — are "blind" (unaware of) whether they receive the active treatment or the placebo treatment. Otherwise, the expectancies of either party could influence the findings.

Appropriate measurement techniques and statistical tests must be built in, so that the entire scientific community can evaluate the findings. Finally, the results must be subjected to the scrutiny of this group. This means that the findings must be published in journals which accept articles for publication only after careful examination by other scientists who have expertise in the particular field.

As if this were not enough, findings are not considered substantive until additional studies have been conducted to reaffirm (or disconfirm) the findings. This process can take years but it allows us to make sound decisions about new treatments.

Alternative Treatments: Another Path

There is also a second path which some practitioners follow, sometimes in an effort to short-cut the longer, more accepted process. This path is fraught with many problems. On this path, proposed treatments stem from concepts which are outside of the mainstream of existing knowledge. They may be instituted long before there is any research which supports their effectiveness — often after only brief, poorly designed trials involving a small number of people. Measurement techniques and statistical means of evaluation are scanty, at best, and often single-case studies are offered as "proof" of the effectiveness of the treatment.

This treatment approach is usually publicized in books or journals which do not require independent review of the material by recognized experts in the field. Often, in fact, the advocate of a particular treatment approach publishes the work. This fact should raise the warning for the consumer-parent. Additionally, although parent support groups have an essential role in the treatment of childhood disorder, in the case of a controversial treatment, parent support groups advocate one and only one treatment. These groups then play an important role in publicizing and promoting that treatment. Unfortunately, enthusiasm is not a substitute for careful scientific investigation.

These alternative interventions commonly claim effectiveness for a broad range of problems. When asked for proof to support these claims, however, proponents are unable to produce documentation. Proponents may also claim to have access to knowledge and information not shared by the medical community at large and, when their treatments are criticized, they may explain this as reflecting a conspiracy against them in the scientific community.

Controversial Treatments for ADHD

Dietary Intervention

Twenty years ago, physician Benjamin Feingold observed that children sensitive to aspirin often had similar reactions to salicylates in foods and to food coloring. Over time, he expanded his elimination diet to include most artificial food flavorings and colorings. Later proponents have also added the preservatives BHA and BHT to the list. Although Feingold's initial hypothesis related the chemicals only to behavior, his theory soon included the claim that these substances were responsible for a broad array of children's learning, behavior and attention problems.

Other advocates of this approach reported that some of the children they treated for allergies showed improvements in activity level, behavior, school work, and even physical symptoms such as muscle pains and headaches. A one-week elimination diet to identify possible offending foods is suggested as part of a treatment approach.

The Evidence

Over the years, advocates of the Feingold Diet have made many dramatic claims.

They state that the additive-free diet will improve most (if not all) children's learning and attention problems and they describe case studies in which children could be removed from drug therapy if their diet was maintained. They also report improvements in school for these children and subsequent deterioration in learning and behavior when the diet is not followed.

In the past fifteen years, dozens of well-controlled studies published in peer-reviewed journals have *consistently failed to find support for Dr. Feingold's approach.* While a few studies have reported some limited success with this approach, at best this suggests that there may be a very small group of children who may be somewhat responsive to additive-free diets.

The lack of well-controlled studies is also true in the case of those who propose a relationship between allergies and behavior or learning problems. Although proponents of this approach may acknowledge that careful scientific studies are necessary, such studies have not yet been conducted. Therefore, they can provide only case studies as supporting evidence for their theory.

"In the past fifteen years, dozens of well-controlled studies published in peer-reviewed journals have consistently failed to find support for Dr. Feingold's approach."

A large number of studies have examined the relationship between sugar and hyperactive behavior, but most of them are difficult to interpret. A few well designed studies have found some effects of sugar on behavior but these effects are very small and only a small percentage of ADHD children seem to be vulnerable.

Conclusion

After careful analysis of the existing evidence, several researchers have concluded that the evidence fails to support a link between diet and children's learning and behavior problems. Of course, like all children, we know that the ADHD child needs a healthy, well-balanced diet. At this time, however, it has not been shown that dietary intervention offers significant help to children with learning and attention problems.

Megavitamins and Mineral Supplements

The use of very high doses of vitamins and minerals to treat ADHD is based on the precepts of orthomolecular psychiatry. Ac-

cording to this theory, some people have a genetic abnormality which results in increased requirements for vitamins and minerals. When these higher-than-normal requirements are not met, various forms of illness result.

In the early 70's, it was claimed that treating hyperactive and learning-disabled children with very high doses of vitamins could decrease hyperactivity and improve attention and concentration. Proponents of this theory also claimed that learning and behavior difficulties are due to deficiencies in minerals such as potassium and sodium, as well as the trace elements such as zinc and copper.

The Evidence

Because vitamins are virtually synonymous with health, this approach has intuitive appeal. The fact that they are "natural" substances also lends them an aura of safety which is reassuring to many people.

The theory also seems "reasonable," since we know that vitamin deficiencies cause an array of serious diseases such as scurvy, pellagra and rickets. Thus, it does not seem far-fetched to hypothesize that vitamin deficiencies could also produce more subtle symptoms such as learning and behavior problems.

In spite of the intuitive appeal of this theory, there is a complete lack of supporting scientific evidence. Dr. Cott's claims are based only on his reported clinical experience and there are no well-controlled studies which support his claims. On the other hand, of three studies in which proper controls *were* employed, none reported positive results. Similarly, there are no controlled studies which support the use of vitamin supplements in the treatment of ADHD.

Conclusion

When vitamins and minerals are used in excessive doses, they can actually be harmful. Too much Vitamin C, for example, can lead to the formation of kidney stones. In 1973, after thorough deliberations, a task force appointed by the American Psychiatric Association concluded that the use of megavitamins to treat behavioral and learning problems was not justified. Three years later, the American Academy of Pediatrics echoed this conclusion. Recent research has not been generated to justify altering these conclusions.

Anti-Motion Sickness Medication

Advocates of this theory believe that ADHD is caused by problems in the inner-ear system. They believe that there is a relationship between ADHD and problems with coordination and balance. This theoretical relationship is thought to reflect a dysfunction in the inner-ear system, since this system plays a major role in balance and coordination.

To treat ADHD, a mixed array of medications including anti-motion sickness medication and several vitamin-like substances are recommended. Using these medications, proponents of this approach claimed a success rate in excess of 90% in a group of 100 ADHD children. Unfortunately, these results are unpublished and so are not subject to verification.

The Evidence

This theory is not consistent in any way with what is currently known about ADHD. There is no body of research that supports a link between the inner-ear system and attentional processes. Anatomically and physiologically, there is no reason to believe that the inner-ear system is involved in attention and impulse control in other than marginal ways. (On the other hand, there are compelling reasons, including documented research findings, to believe that attention and impulse control are regulated through frontal and other systems in the brain.)

Advocates of this model have yet to provide scientific support from well controlled investigations. Instead, anecdotal evidence and single-case studies are offered to suggest that this treatment is effective. As many treatment have followed the short-cut path, advocates of this approach caution that we should not expect to read about this work in the scientific literature since researchers have overlooked and unfairly discounted this theory.

In the single controlled study of this theory, researchers evaluated the use of anti-motion sickness medication to treat developmental reading disorders. The results failed to support the theory.

Conclusion

This approach to treating ADHD is inconsistent with current knowledge concerning the condition and is not supported by research findings. At this time, it should not be used in the treatment of ADHD.

Candida Yeast

Candida albicans is a type of yeast which lives in the human body. Normally, yeast growth is kept in check by a strong immune system and by "friendly" bacteria in the body. When the immune system is weakened or when friendly bacteria are killed by antibiotics, Candida can overgrow. This may lead to the vaginal yeast infection known as Candidiasis and, less commonly, infections of the skin, nails and mouth.

Those who support this model believe that toxins produced by yeast overgrowth weaken the immune system. This makes

the body susceptible to many illnesses, including ADHD and other psychiatric disorders.

This treatment program is designed to discourage the growth of Candida in the body. The two-pronged approach includes antifungal medication, such as nystatin (to kill yeasts without harming friendly bacteria), and a low-sugar diet (since sugar is believed to stimulate yeast growth).

Other aspects of this treatment program are an elimination diet to rule out food allergies and the use of vitamin and mineral supplements. Since proponents believe that people with yeast-related problems are also likely to be susceptible to chemicals and molds, they suggest tests to identify these sensitivities so the offending substances can be avoided.

The Evidence

Although we know that Candida can cause infections of the vagina, mouth and skin, there is little evidence to support the idea that it also causes the host of other illnesses listed by advocates of this approach. These ideas are not consistent with what is currently known about the causes of ADHD.

Little evidence is provided to support these theories. Instead, anecdotal data and testimonials are offered as proof that the approach is effective. There is no evidence from controlled studies which supports this model. In fact, there may be no way to test this theory at all, since supporters claim that such a multitude of factors are associated with Candida-related illness that no investigator could possibly control for so many factors.

Conclusion

This theory is not supported by evidence. Until it has been subjected to rigorous investigation, it should not be employed in the treatment of ADHD.

EEG Biofeedback

Proponents of this approach believe that ADHD children can be trained to increase the type of brain-wave activity associated with sustained attention and to decrease the type of activity associated with daydreaming and distraction. They claim the result is improvement in attention and reductions in hyperactivity and impulsivity.

The technique of EEG biofeedback involves measuring levels of electrical activity in various regions of the brain. This information is fed into a computer, which transforms it into a signal, such as a light or tone. Using this signal as "feedback," the child is taught to increase certain kinds of brain-wave activity and decrease other kinds. With children, the method usually involves a reward system, such that the

child earns points or tokens for increasing desired brain-wave activity. Training usually involves between 40 and 80 treatment sessions, each lasting up to 40 minutes or more. Since sessions are held two to three times per week, treatment can extend over three to ten months, or longer. In one popular program, biofeedback is often combined with a program of academic tutoring.

The Evidence

As supporters of this approach point out, the theory underlying EEG biofeedback as a treatment for ADHD is consistent with what is known about low levels of arousal in frontal brain areas in people with ADHD. There have also been a few studies which have shown impressive results for this method. Specifically, the ADHD children who were studied quickly learned to increase the desired brain wave activity. Parent and teacher rating scales showed considerable behavioral improvement and scores on IQ tests and achievement tests also improved dramatically.

These studies are seriously flawed by the use of small numbers of children with ambiguous diagnoses. Furthermore, these studies have not included appropriate control groups to rule out the effects of maturation or — more importantly — the placebo effect. Biofeedback has the potential to produce significant placebo effects because it is an impressive, high-tech procedure that provides a great deal of individual attention to the child.

"Similarly, there are no controlled studies which support the use of vitamin supplements in the treatment of ADHD."

Conclusion

Biofeedback technology is not new. When it first appeared in the 1960's, it was hailed as a promising treatment for a host of human illnesses and problems. Scientists were understandably excited by the idea that people could gain control over bodily processes and, literally, learn not to be sick.

Biofeedback, however, has not proven to be a generally effective treatment for a wide range of problems. Today it is an ancillary treatment that is used in support of other treatments. It provides documented benefits for pain management but the symptom relief it offers is often no greater than the relief provided by simple relaxation or hypnotherapy methods.

The application of biofeedback technology to the treatment of ADHD is unproven and parents are advised to proceed with caution. It is an expensive approach whose effectiveness, until better studies have been completed, is not demonstrated at this time.

Other Controversial Treatments

Applied Kinesiology

This chiropractic method is also known as the Neural Organization Technique. According to proponents of this approach, learning disabilities are caused by the mis-alignment of two specific bones in the skull, the sphenoid and the temporal bones. This mis-alignment, they say, creates unequal pressure on different areas of the brain, leading to brain malfunction. Misalignment of these bones also creates a problem they call "ocular lock," an eye-movement malfunction which contributes to reading problems. They also discuss pelvic reflexes which, if not synchronized, impair the chemical and mechanical functioning of the body.

Treatment consists of restoring the cranial bones to their proper position through specific bodily manipulations. Once this has supposedly been accomplished, the individual is capable of learning but, since there is a need to catch up on what he did not have the opportunity to learn before treatment, remedial tutoring is included as part of the treatment program.

The Evidence

This theory is not consistent with what is currently known about the cause of learning disabilities. It is also not consistent with what is known about human anatomy, since standard medical textbooks state that cranial bones do not move. No research has been done to support the effectiveness of this form of treatment. In individual cases in which improvement may have occurred, the improvement in academic performance could well be attributed to remedial tutoring.

Conclusion

In all respects, this approach to treating learning disabilities is far outside the mainstream of current thought and clinical practice. It has no place in the treatment of learning-disabled children.

Optometric Vision Training

An optometrist is specifically trained to test visual acuity and prescribe corrective lenses for visual problems. A group of optometrists offering a sub-specialty referred to as behavioral optometry have proposed the idea that reading disorders are caused by visual problems such as faulty eye movements, sensitivity of the eyes to certain light frequencies, and failure of the eyes to focus together.

Vision treatment programs are extremely varied in terms of the components which are included. Some, for example, concentrate on a program of eye exercises designed to improve the ability of the eyes to move smoothly and focus together. In other programs, the child is fitted with colored lenses. Educational and perceptual training techniques may also be employed. In still other training programs, adjunctive procedures such as biofeedback, nutritional counseling and family therapy may be used.

The Evidence

The idea that visual disorders underlie reading problems has intuitive appeal because of the obvious role of vision in the reading process. However, investigators in the fields of education, psychology and neuropsychology have concluded that most reading disorders are not caused by visual processing disorders. Instead, they are due to deficiencies in the storage and retrieval of linguistic information.

There is some evidence that poor readers show differences in back-tracking and stop-and-start movements of the eyes during reading. It is likely that these differences reflect reading problems rather than cause them, since the same patterns can be produced in competent readers simply by increasing the complexity of the material.

Scientific studies of this approach are few in number and flawed in design. Several reviewers have concluded that there is no evidence that these programs are effective in treating reading disorders. In 1972, a joint statement highly critical of the optometric approach was issued by the American Academy of Pediatrics, the American Academy of Ophthalmology and Otolaryngology, and the American Asso-

---

"There is no body of research that supports a link between the inner-ear system and attentional processes."

---

ciation of Ophthalmology (a statement later supported by the American Association for Pediatric Ophthalmology and Strabismus).

Conclusion

In the absence of supporting evidence for the effectiveness of optometric training, it should not be employed in the treatment of learning disabilities.

SUMMARY

In this paper, we have reviewed approaches which have been offered as effective for ADHD but which have not met scientific standards which would justify their inclusion as mainstream treatments for this childhood disorder. As we noted, some of these controversial treatments merit continued research, while others do not.

Although these treatments may be offered as proven and accepted approaches for ADHD, they are not. We caution parents who are considering these treatments that time and money might be better spent on treatments with proven track records. Among the most effective methods to date are the judicious use of medication and behavior management. In addition, when cognitive self-control programs are applied carefully and consistently and with opportunities for new learning to generalize, they can also be helpful. Finally, of course, parent education is an essential component of an effective treatment program, as it is with any childhood disorder.

How Can A Parent Be A Wise Consumer?

If you are the parent of a child with ADHD and/or learning disabilities, you know how difficult your job can be. Of course, you want to obtain the very best treatment for your child. In a spirit of "How can it hurt to try it?" you might be tempted to throw caution to the wind when you hear about a new treatment that promises to help.

But promises are not enough. You also have the responsibility to invest your family's resources of time, money and energy wisely. This means that you must become an informed consumer.

In this paper, we have provided general guidelines for evaluating new treatments. Listed below are some additional tips to help you recognize treatments that are questionable.

- Overstatement and exaggerated claims are "red flags." Be suspicious of any product or treatment that is described as "astonishing," "miraculous," or "an amazing breakthrough." Legitimate health professionals do not use words like these, nor do they boast of their success in treating huge numbers of patients.
- Be suspicious, too, of any treatment that claims to treat a wide variety of ailments. Common sense tells us that the more grandiose the claim, the less likely it is that there is any real merit behind it.
- Do not rely on testimonials from people who say they have been helped by the product or the treatment. Enthusiasm is not substitute for evidence and legitimate health professionals do not solicit testimonials from their patients.
- Be skeptical about claims that a treatment is being suppressed or unfairly attacked by the medical establishment. Legitimate health professionals eagerly welcome new knowledge and better methods of treatment for their patients. They have no reason to suppress or oppose promising new approaches.

CH.A.D.D. Membership

☐ **Yes!** I would like to become a member of CH.A.D.D. and receive:

- CHADDER, our bi-annual newsletter
- CHADDer Box, our monthly newsletter
- Monthly support group meetings
- Informed discussion groups with local professionals
- Current information on ADD
- Tips for teachers
- Support network from other parents

CHAPTER NAME: _____

I heard of CH.A.D.D. through: _____

I believe I can help in the following way(s): _____
_____

My occupation is: _____

Name: _____

Address: _____

City: _____ State: _____ Zip: _____ Telephone: _____

I have enclosed my annual membership dues. Annual membership runs twelve months from the month joined.

☐ $ 30.00 — Family Membership
☐ $ 60.00 — Professional Membership
☐ $100.00 — International Membership
   (Persons living outside continental U.S. and Canada)
☐ I would like to make an additional contribution of:
                              $ _____
          Enclosed is $ _____

Count me as a CH.A.D.D. member.
I am interested in Attention Deficit Disorders as a:
☐ parent   ☐ adult   ☐ doctor   ☐ teacher
☐ health-care professional   ☐ other _____

Organizational Membership Form

For schools, counseling and educational centers, professional offices and hospitals we now offer an Organizational Membership in CH.A.D.D. Join now and receive:

- 20 copies of CHADDER bi-annually
- 20 copies of the CH.A.D.D. Teacher's Guide
- Announcements of informative monthly meetings
- Current information on ADD • Tips for teachers
- 20 copies of CHADDer Box monthly
- Certificate of Membership in CH.A.D.D.
- Informed discussion groups with local professionals
- Announcements of regional & national conferences

We have enclosed our annual organizational membership dues. Annual membership runs twelve months from the month joined.

_____ $150.00 Organizational Membership (Signed Purchase Orders Accepted)

Name of Institution _____

Contact Person _____

Address _____

City _____ State _____ Zip _____ Telephone _____

Detach and mail to: / Children with Attention Deficit Disorders
          499 Northwest 70th Avenue, Suite 308, Plantation, Florida 33317
          (305) 587-3700 • (305) 587-4599 Fax

EDUCATORS MANUAL ORDER FORM

For additional copies of **THE CH.A.D.D. EDUCATORS MANUAL** mail orders to: **CASET ASSOCIATES**, 3927 Old Lee Highway, Fairfax, VA 22030 or phone: (800) 545-5583 or FAX (703) 352-2405.

_____ Individual manuals: $10.00 each plus $2.00 shipping and handling $_____

_____ Bulk Order: 1 case (25 manuals per case): $150.00 plus $20.00 shipping and handling $_____

                                                              TOTAL $_____

Make checks payable to **CASET ASSOCIATES**. (Purchase orders accepted for orders of $150 or more.)

PAYMENT: ☐ Check   ☐ Credit Card (MasterCard/VISA)
             ☐ Cash   Card Number ☐☐☐☐☐☐☐☐☐☐☐☐☐☐☐☐☐☐☐☐
             ☐ Purchase Order Expiration Date ____ / ____

Name _____   Signature _____

Company Name _____   Phone Number (____) _____

Address _____ City _____ State _____ Zip _____

EDUCATORS MANUAL ORDER FORM

For additional copies of **THE CH.A.D.D. EDUCATORS MANUAL** mail orders to: **CASET ASSOCIATES**, 3927 Old Lee Highway, Fairfax, VA 22030 or phone: (800) 545-5583 or FAX (703) 352-2405.

_____ Individual manuals: $10.00 each plus $2.00 shipping and handling $_____

_____ Bulk Order: 1 case (25 manuals per case): $150.00 plus $20.00 shipping and handling $_____

TOTAL $_____

Make checks payable to **CASET ASSOCIATES**. (Purchase orders accepted for orders of $150 or more.)

PAYMENT: ☐ Check   ☐ Credit Card (MasterCard/VISA)
                 ☐ Cash   Card Number ☐☐☐☐☐☐☐☐☐☐☐☐☐☐☐☐☐☐☐
                 ☐ Purchase Order Expiration Date ____ / ____

Name_____   Signature_____
Company Name_____   Phone Number (____) _____
Address_____ City_____ State_____ Zip_____

EDUCATORS MANUAL ORDER FORM

For additional copies of **THE CH.A.D.D. EDUCATORS MANUAL** mail orders to: **CASET ASSOCIATES**, 3927 Old Lee Highway, Fairfax, VA 22030 or phone: (800) 545-5583 or FAX (703) 352-2405.

_____ Individual manuals: $10.00 each plus $2.00 shipping and handling $_____

_____ Bulk Order: 1 case (25 manuals per case): $150.00 plus $20.00 shipping and handling $_____

TOTAL $_____

Make checks payable to **CASET ASSOCIATES**. (Purchase orders accepted for orders of $150 or more.)

PAYMENT: ☐ Check   ☐ Credit Card (MasterCard/VISA)
                 ☐ Cash   Card Number ☐☐☐☐☐☐☐☐☐☐☐☐☐☐☐☐☐☐☐
                 ☐ Purchase Order Expiration Date ____ / ____

Name_____   Signature_____
Company Name_____   Phone Number (____) _____
Address_____ City_____ State_____ Zip_____

EDUCATORS MANUAL ORDER FORM

For additional copies of **THE CH.A.D.D. EDUCATORS MANUAL** mail orders to: **CASET ASSOCIATES**, 3927 Old Lee Highway, Fairfax, VA 22030 or phone: (800) 545-5583 or FAX (703) 352-2405.

_____ Individual manuals: $10.00 each plus $2.00 shipping and handling $_____

_____ Bulk Order: 1 case (25 manuals per case): $150.00 plus $20.00 shipping and handling $_____

TOTAL $_____

Make checks payable to **CASET ASSOCIATES**. (Purchase orders accepted for orders of $150 or more.)

PAYMENT: ☐ Check   ☐ Credit Card (MasterCard/VISA)
                 ☐ Cash   Card Number ☐☐☐☐☐☐☐☐☐☐☐☐☐☐☐☐☐☐☐
                 ☐ Purchase Order Expiration Date ____ / ____

Name_____   Signature_____
Company Name_____   Phone Number (____) _____
Address_____ City_____ State_____ Zip_____